INTRODUCING PSYCHOLOGY

HOW TO STOP PROCRASTINATION ANDDISCOVER POSITIVE THINKING, MOTIVATION AND CONFIDENCE

By

Daniel Anderson

TABLE OF CONTENTS

HISTORY OF PHSYCOLOGY

It is always a difficult question to ask, where to begin to tell the story of the history of psychology. Some would start with ancient Greece; others would look to a demarcation in the late 19th century when the science of psychology was formally proposed and instituted. These two perspectives, and all that is in between, are appropriate for describing a history of psychology. The interested student will have no trouble finding an abundance of resources on all of these time frames and perspectives (Goodwin, 2011; Leahey, 2012; Schultz & Schultz, 2007). For the purposes of this module, we will examine the development of psychology in America and use the mid-19th century as our starting point. For the sake of convenience, we refer to this as a history of modern psychology.

Psychology is an exciting field and the history of psychology offers the opportunity to make sense of how it has grown and developed. The history of psychology also provides perspective. Rather than a dry collection of names and dates, the history of psychology tells us about the important intersection of time and place that defines who we are. Consider what happens when you meet someone for the first time. The conversation usually begins with a series of questions such as, "Where did you grow up?" "How long have you lived here?" "Where did you go to school?" The importance of history in defining who we are cannot be overstated. Whether you are seeing a physician, talking with a counselor, or applying for a job, everything begins with a history. The same is true for studying the history of psychology; getting a history of the field helps to make sense of where we are and how we got here.

A Prehistory Of Psychology

Precursors to American psychology can be found in philosophy and physiology. Philosophers such as John Locke (1632–1704) and Thomas Reid (1710–1796) promoted empiricism, the idea that all knowledge comes from experience. The work of Locke, Reid, and others emphasized the role of the human observer and the primacy of the senses in defining how the mind comes to acquire knowledge. In American colleges and universities in the early 1800s, these principles were taught as courses on mental and moral philosophy. Most often these courses taught about the mind based on the faculties of intellect, will, and the senses (Fuchs, 2000).

Physiology And Psychophysics

Philosophical questions about the nature of mind and

knowledge were matched in the 19th century by physiological investigations of the sensory systems of the human observer. German physiologist Hermann von Helmholtz (1821–1894) measured the speed of the neural impulse and explored the physiology of hearing and vision. His work indicated that our senses can deceive us and are not a mirror of the external world. Such work showed that even though the human senses were fallible, the mind could be measured using the methods of science. In all, it suggested that a science of psychology was feasible.

An important implication of Helmholtz's work was that there is a psychological reality and a physical reality and that the two are not identical. This was not a new idea; philosophers like John Locke had written extensively on the topic, and in the 19th century, philosophical speculation about the nature of mind became subject to the rigors of science.

The question of the relationship between the mental (experiences of the senses) and the material (external reality) was investigated by a number of German researchers including Ernst Weber and Gustav Fechner. Their work was called psychophysics, and it introduced methods for measuring the relationship between physical stimuli and human perception that would serve as the basis for the new science of psychology (Fancher & Rutherford, 2011).

Wilhelm Wundt

The formal development of modern psychology is usually credited to the work of German physician, physiologist, and philosopher Wilhelm Wundt (1832–1920). Wundt helped to establish the field of experimental psychology by serving as a strong promoter of the idea that psychology could be an experimental field and by providing classes, textbooks, and a laboratory for training students. In 1875, he joined the faculty at the University of Leipzig and quickly began to make plans for the creation of a program of experimental psychology. In 1879, he complemented his lectures on experimental psychology with a laboratory experience: an event that has served as the popular date for the establishment of the science of psychology.

The response to the new science was immediate and global. Wundt attracted students from around the world to study the new experimental psychology and work in his lab. Students were trained to offer detailed self-reports of their reactions to various stimuli, a procedure known as introspection. The goal was to identify the elements of consciousness. In addition to the study of sensation and perception, research was done on mental chronometry, more commonly known as reaction time. The work of Wundt and his students demonstrated that the mind could be measured and the nature of consciousness could be revealed through scientific means. It was an exciting proposition, and one that found great interest in America. After the opening of Wundt's lab in 1879, it took just four years for the first psychology laboratory to open in the United States (Benjamin, 2007).

Scientific Psychology Comes to the United States

Wundt's version of psychology arrived in America most visibly through the work of Edward Bradford Titchener (1867–1927). A student of Wundt's, Titchener brought to America a brand of experimental psychology referred to as "structuralism." Structuralists were interested in the contents of the mind—what the mind is. For Titchener, the general adult mind was the proper focus for the new psychology, and he excluded from study those with mental deficiencies, children, and animals (Evans, 1972; Titchener, 1909).

Experimental psychology spread rather rapidly throughout North America. By 1900, there were more than 40 laboratories in the United States and Canada (Benjamin, 2000). Psychology in America also organized early with the establishment of the American Psychological Association (APA) in 1892. Titchener felt that this new organization did not adequately represent the interests of experimental psychology, so, in 1904, he organized a group of colleagues to create what is now known as the Society of Experimental Psychologists (Goodwin, 1985). The group met annually to discuss research in experimental psychology. Reflecting the times, women researchers were not invited (or welcome). It is interesting to note that Titchener's first doctoral student was a woman, Margaret Floy Washburn (1871–1939). Despite many barriers, in 1894, Washburn became the first woman in America to earn a Ph.D. in psychology and, in 1921, only the second woman to be elected president of the American Psychological Association (Scarborough & Furumoto, 1987).

Striking a balance between the science and practice of psychology continues to this day. In 1988, the American Psychological Society (now known as the Association for Psychological Science) was founded with the central mission of advancing psychological science.

Toward A Functional Psychology

William James was one of the leading figures in a new perspective on psychology called functionalism.

While Titchener and his followers adhered to a

structural psychology, others in America were pursuing different approaches. William James, G. Stanley Hall, and James McKeen Cattell were among a group that became identified with "functionalism." Influenced by Darwin's evolutionary theory, functionalists were interested in the activities of the mind—what the mind does. An interest in functionalism opened the way for the study of a wide range of approaches, including animal and comparative psychology (Benjamin, 2007).

William James (1842–1910) is regarded as writing perhaps the most influential and important book in the field of psychology, Principles of Psychology, published in 1890. Opposed to the reductionist ideas of Titchener, James proposed that consciousness is ongoing and continuous; it cannot be isolated and reduced to elements. For James, consciousness helped us adapt to our environment in such ways as allowing us to make choices and have personal responsibility over those choices.

At Harvard, James occupied a position of authority and respect in psychology and philosophy. Through his teaching and writing, he influenced psychology for generations. One of his students, Mary Whiton Calkins (1863–1930), faced many of the challenges that confronted Margaret Floy Washburn and other women interested in pursuing graduate education in psychology. With much persistence, Calkins was able to study with James at Harvard. She eventually completed all the requirements for the doctoral degree, but Harvard refused to grant her a diploma because she was a woman. Despite these challenges, Calkins went on to become an accomplished researcher and the first woman elected president of the American Psychological Association in 1905 (Scarborough & Furumoto, 1987).

G. Stanley Hall (1844–1924) made substantial and lasting contributions to the establishment of psychology in the United States. At Johns Hopkins University, he founded the first psychological laboratory in America in 1883. In 1887, he created the first journal of psychology in America, American Journal of Psychology. In 1892, he founded the American Psychological Association (APA); in 1909, he invited and hosted Freud at Clark University (the only time Freud visited America). Influenced by evolutionary theory, Hall was interested in the process of adaptation and human development. Using surveys and questionnaires to study children, Hall wrote extensively on child development and education. While graduate education in psychology was restricted for women in Hall's time, it was all but non-existent for African Americans. In another first,

Hall mentored Francis Cecil Sumner (1895–1954) who, in 1920, became the first African American to earn a Ph.D. in psychology in America (Guthrie, 2003).

James McKeen Cattell (1860–1944) received his Ph.D. with Wundt but quickly turned his interests to the assessment of individual differences. Influenced by the work of Darwin's cousin, Frances Galton, Cattell believed that mental abilities such as intelligence were inherited and could be measured using mental tests. Like Galton, he believed society was better served by identifying those with superior intelligence and supported efforts to encourage them to reproduce. Such beliefs were associated with eugenics (the promotion of selective breeding) and fueled early debates about the contributions of heredity and environment in defining who we are. At Columbia University, Cattell developed a department of psychology that became world famous also promoting psychological science through advocacy and as a publisher of scientific journals and reference works (Fancher, 1987; Sokal, 1980).

The Growth Of Psychology

Throughout the first half of the 20th century, psychology continued to grow and flourish in America. It was large enough to accommodate varying points of view on the nature of mind and behavior. Gestalt psychology is a good example. The Gestalt movement began in Germany with the work of Max Wertheimer (1880–1943). Opposed to the reductionist approach of Wundt's laboratory psychology, Wertheimer and his colleagues Kurt Koffka (1886–1941), Wolfgang Kohler (1887–1967), and Kurt Lewin (1890–1947) believed that studying the whole of any experience was richer than studying individual aspects of that experience. The saying "the whole is greater than the sum of its parts" is a Gestalt perspective. Consider that a melody is an additional element beyond the collection of notes that comprise it. The Gestalt psychologists proposed that the mind often processes information simultaneously rather than sequentially. For instance, when you look at a photograph, you see a whole image, not just a collection of pixels of color. Using Gestalt principles, Wertheimer and his colleagues also explored the nature of learning and thinking. Most of the German Gestalt psychologists were Jewish and were forced to flee the Nazi regime due to the threats posed on both academic and personal freedoms. In America, they were able to introduce a new audience to the Gestalt perspective, demonstrating how it could be applied to perception and learning (Wertheimer, 1938). In many ways, the work of the Gestalt psychologists served as a precursor to the rise of cognitive psychology in America (Benjamin, 2007).

Behaviorism emerged early in the 20th century and became a major force in American psychology. Championed by psychologists such as John B. Watson (1878–1958) and B. F. Skinner (1904–1990), behaviorism rejected any reference to mind and viewed overt and observable behavior as the proper subject matter of psychology. Through the scientific study of behavior, it was hoped that laws of learning could be derived that would promote the prediction and control of behavior. Russian physiologist Ivan Pavlov (1849–1936) influenced early behaviorism in America. His work on conditioned learning, popularly referred to as classical conditioning, provided support for the notion that learning and behavior were controlled by events in the environment and could be explained with no reference to mind or consciousness (Fancher, 1987).

For decades, behaviorism dominated American psychology. By the 1960s, psychologists began to recognize that behaviorism was unable to fully explain human behavior because it neglected mental processes. The turn toward a cognitive psychology was not new. In the 1930s, British psychologist Frederic C. Bartlett (1886–1969) explored the idea of the constructive mind, recognizing that people use their past experiences to construct frameworks in which to understand new experiences. Some of the major pioneers in American cognitive psychology include Jerome Bruner (1915–), Roger Brown (1925–1997), and George Miller (1920–2012). In the 1950s, Bruner conducted pioneering studies on cognitive aspects of sensation and perception. Brown conducted original research on language and memory, coined the term "flashbulb memory," and figured out how to study the tip-of-the-tongue phenomenon (Benjamin, 2007). Miller's research on working memory is legendary. His 1956 paper "The Magic Number Seven, Plus or Minus Two: Some Limits on Our Capacity for Processing Information"is one of the most highly cited papers in psychology. A popular interpretation of Miller's research was that the number of bits of information an average human can hold in working memory is 7 ± 2. Around the same time, the study of computer science was growing and was used as an analogy to explore and understand how the mind works. The work of Miller and others in the 1950s and 1960s has inspired tremendous interest in cognition and neuroscience, both of which dominate much of contemporary American psychology.

Psychology And Society

Given that psychology deals with the human condition, it is not surprising that psychologists would involve themselves in social issues. For more than a century, psychology and psychologists have been agents of social action and change. Using the methods and tools of science, psychologists have challenged assumptions, stereotypes, and stigma. Founded in 1936, the Society for the Psychological Study of Social Issues (SPSSI) has supported research and action on a wide range of social issues. Individually, there have been many psychologists whose efforts have promoted social change. Helen Thompson Woolley (1874–1947) and Leta S. Hollingworth (1886–1939) were pioneers in research on the psychology of sex differences. Working in the early 20th century, when women's rights were marginalized, Thompson examined the assumption that women were overemotional compared to men and found that emotion did not influence women's decisions any more than it did men's. Hollingworth found that menstruation did not negatively impact women's cognitive or motor abilities. Such work combatted harmful stereotypes and showed that psychological research could contribute to social change (Scarborough & Furumoto, 1987).

Among the first generation of African American

psychologists, Mamie Phipps Clark (1917–1983) and her husband Kenneth Clark (1914–2005) studied the psychology of race and demonstrated the ways in which school segregation negatively impacted the self-esteem of African American children. Their research was influential in the 1954 Supreme Court ruling in the case of Brown v. Board of Education, which ended school segregation (Guthrie, 2003). In psychology, greater advocacy for issues impacting the African American community were advanced by the creation of the Association of Black Psychologists (ABPsi) in 1968.

In 1957, psychologist Evelyn Hooker (1907–1996) published the paper "The Adjustment of the Male Overt Homosexual," reporting on her research that showed no significant differences in psychological adjustment between homosexual and heterosexual men. Her research helped to de-pathologize homosexuality and contributed to the decision by the American Psychiatric Association to remove homosexuality from the Diagnostic and Statistical Manual of Mental Disorders in 1973 (Garnets & Kimmel, 2003).

WHAT IS PHSYCOLOGY

Psychology has evolved from the Greek word "psyche," which means "soul" or "mind," and "logos," which means speech. It is an academic and applied field concerning the study of the mind, brain, and behavior, both human and nonhuman. Psychology also refers to the practical application of such knowledge to diverse spheres of human activity, including problems of people's daily lives and the treatment of psychological illness.

In simple words, psychology involves study of the human mind and how it functions in different situations. In other words, basically it involves a deep analysis of how people think, behave and interact with one another in different type of situations and environments. This subject traces its roots to ancient civilizations of India, Egypt, China and Greece. Wilhelm Wundt, a German Doctor is the person responsible for bringing psychology into lab settings and also introducing the structural school of psychology. After that many eminent researchers and analysts have contributed a lot in this field as it is never possible to read and predict the human mind in totality. Perhaps this is something that can change even before you may imagine. That's the main beauty of this field because it deals with the most complex thing on the earth i.e. human mind.

Various approaches to psychology include forensic, abnormal, computational, developmental, cognitive and quantitative psychology. Psychologists make use of three types of inferences which are deduction, induction and abduction to provide explanations on the way the mind works. As part of their efforts to understand the way the mind works, they make use of survey results. Surveys are used to record data which are needed to measure mood change patterns, attitude and traits, and other aspects of the human mind.

Psychology has evolved from the Greek word "psyche," which means "soul" or "mind," and "logos," which means speech. It is an academic and applied field concerning the study of the mind, brain, and behavior, both human and nonhuman. Psychology also refers to the practical application of such knowledge to diverse spheres of human activity, including problems of people's daily lives and the treatment of psychological illness.

Psychology differs from anthropology, economics, political science, and sociology in seeking to capture illustrative generalizations about the mental function and explicit behavior of individuals. However, contrary to this, other disciplines depend more heavily on field studies and historical methods for extracting expressive generalizations. In reality, however, there is much "cross-fertilization" that takes place among different fields. Psychology differs from biology and neuroscience in that it is mainly concerned with the interface between mental processes and behavior of a person. It also refers to the common procedures of a system and not merely the biological or neural procedures themselves.

However, subfields of psychology, such as neuropsychology, combine the study of the actual neural processes with the study of the mental effects they have intuitively produced. Psychology in literal terms means the study of the human mind. It illustrates and attempts to explain awareness, behavior, and social interaction. This study can be structured purely in terms of phenomenological descriptions of internal experiences or as a result of behavior, which includes social conduct. Empirical psychology is mainly dedicated to describing human experience and behavior as it actually occurs.

The study of the correlation between consciousness and the brain or nervous system has been undertaken only recently. However, it is still not clear in what ways they interact.

Psychology is a particularly extensive field, which includes various approaches to the study of mental processes and behavior. An understanding of brain function is gradually being included in psychological theory and practice, particularly in areas such as artificial intelligence, neuropsychological, and cognitive neuroscience. Mechanical and electronic computing has played an important role in developing the information-processing hypothesis of the mind.

Importance Of Psychology

Psychology is very important especially because it deals with the study of the mental processes and behaviour at the same time. It is also applied in our daily lives and in many things

There are many misconceptions regarding the field of psychology, especially because of its diversity and the different careers associated with the study of psychology. Psychology is actually a science and a discipline in both academic and applied field which deals with the human mind and its relation to human behaviour. The aim of psychology is to understand, explain, and predict the thought, emotion, and the behaviour of man. Psychology is involved in various areas of study and application in different subjects.

Psychology is very important especially because it deals with the study of the mental processes and behaviour at the same time. It is also applied in our daily lives and in many things. How we behave, how we react to situations, and how we perform are all associated with psychology. That is because psychology studies our nature, how we think and how it is related to what we do, and why we think and act the way we do. It is actually very complicated because unlike the study of disease processes and the physical body, studying the human mind is very complicated and it is hard to study in an unbiased way. Its importance in the society has grown significantly over the years. Psychology is used to study various kinds of mental and life threatening diseases such as in Alzheimer's, Parkinson's, and many other types of neurological disorders. Psychology is also used to better understand and help those with pervasive developmental disorders such as autism. The study of psychology in these disorders and diseases has helped the medical professionals in developing cure and treatment for certain diseases.

With psychology, we are able to learn about ourselves. To fully understand ourselves we have to know about the causes of our own behaviour and our perspectives in life. By knowing ourselves and learning our own personality, we can develop goals for ourselves. Also, by learning about ourselves, we are able to learn about other people and their differences. Gaining understanding of oneself and of others can help improve the way relationships and communications work. These are only some of the common uses and the importance of studying psychology.

Psychology allows people to understand more about how the body and mind work together. This knowledge can help with decision-making and avoiding stressful situations. It can help with time management, setting and achieving goals, and living effectively.

The science not only allows people to be more successful, but it can also impact their health. It helps many tackle their mental illnesses so that they can continue living their lives. Psychological studies have also aided in drug development and the ability to diagnose various diseases (such as Alzheimer's and Parkinson's).

I can personally testify to the importance of the subject. Psychology has helped me as a writer because I have become more determined to do the things I will enjoy and write on the topics that I like. I can understand who I am and look at events on a more positive aspect. Whenever I have a problem, I can handle it better. Down to the choices over the projects I will work on and the way I will handle my time, psychology helps me make better decisions within my life.

HOW PSYCHOLOGYCAN HELP YOU LIVE A BETTER LIFE

How can psychology apply to your everyday life? Do you think that psychology is just for students, academics, and therapists? Then think again. Because psychology is both an applied and a theoretical subject, it can be utilized in a number of ways.

While research studies aren't exactly light reading material for the average person, the results of these experiments and studies can have significant applications in daily life. The following are some of the top ten practical uses for psychology in everyday life.

Get Motivated

Whether your goal is to quit smoking, lose weight, or learn a new language, some lessons from psychology offer tips for getting motivated. To increase your motivational levels when approaching a task, utilize some of the following tips derived from research in cognitive and educational psychology:

- ✓ Introduce new or novel elements to keep your interest high

- ✓ Vary the sequence to help stave off boredom

✓ Learn new things that build on your existing knowledge

✓ Set clear goals that are directly related to the task

✓ Reward yourself for a job well done

Improve Your Leadership Skills

It doesn't matter if you're an office manager or a volunteer at a local youth group, having good leadership skills will probably be essential at some point in your life. Not everyone is a born leader, but a few simple tips gleaned from psychological research can help you improve your leadership skills.

One of the most famous studies on this topic looked at three distinct leadership styles. Based on the findings of this study and subsequent research, practice some of the following when you are in a leadership position:

✓ Offer clear guidance, but allow group members to voice opinions

✓ Talk about possible solutions to problems with members of the group

✓ Focus on stimulating ideas and be willing to reward creativity

Become A Better Communicator

Communication involves much more than how you speak or write. Research suggests that nonverbal signals make up a huge portion of our interpersonal communications. To communicate your message effectively, you need to learn how to express yourself nonverbally and to read the nonverbal cues of those around you.

✓ A few key strategies include the following:

✓ Use good eye contact

✓ Start noticing nonverbal signals in others

✓ Learn to use your tone of voice to reinforce your message

Learn To Better Understand Others

Much like nonverbal communication, your ability to understand your emotions and the emotions of those around you plays an important role in your relationships and professional life. The term emotional intelligence refers to your ability to understand both your own emotions as well as those of other people.

Your emotional intelligence quotient is a measure of this ability. According to psychologist Daniel Goleman, your EQ may actually be more important than your IQ.

What can you do to become more emotionally intelligent? Consider some of the following strategies:

✓ Carefully assess your own emotional reactions

✓ Record your experience and emotions in a journal

✓ Try to see situations from the perspective of another person

Make More Accurate Decisions

Research in cognitive psychology has provided a wealth of information about decision making. By applying these strategies to your life, you can learn to make wiser choices. The next time you need to make a big decision, try using some of the following techniques:

Try using the "six thinking hats" approach by looking at the situation from multiple points of view, including rational, emotional, intuitive, creative, positive, and negative perspectives

Consider the potential costs and benefits of a decision

Employ a grid analysis technique that gives a score for how a particular decision will satisfy specific requirements you may have

Improve Your Memory

Have you ever wondered why you can remember exact details of childhood events yet forget the name of the new client you met yesterday? Research on how we form new memories as well as how and why we forget has led to a number of findings that can be applied directly in your daily life.

What are some ways you can increase your memory power?

- ✓ Focus on the information.

- ✓ Rehearse what you have learned.

- ✓ Eliminate distractions.

Make Wiser Financial Decisions

Nobel Prize-winning psychologist Daniel Kahneman and his colleague Amos Tversky conducted a series of studies that looked at how people manage uncertainty and risk when making decisions. Subsequent research in this area known as behavior economics has yielded some key findings that you can use to make wiser money management choices.

One study found that workers could more than triple their savings by utilizing some of the following strategies:

- ✓ Don't procrastinate. Start investing in savings now

- ✓ Commit in advance to devote portions of your future earnings to your retirement savings

- ✓ Try to be aware of personal biases that may lead to poor money choices

Get Better Grades

The next time you're tempted to complain about pop quizzes, midterms, or final exams, consider this;research has demonstrated that taking tests actually helps you better remember what you've learned, even if it wasn't covered on the test.

Another study found that repeated test-taking may be a better memory aid than studying. Students who were tested repeatedly were able to recall 61 percent of the material while those in the study group recalled only 40 percent. How can you apply these findings to your own life? When trying to learn new information, self-test frequently in order to cement what you have learned into your memory.

Become More Productive

Sometimes it seems like there are thousands of books, blogs, and magazine articles telling us how to get more done in a day, but how much of this advice is founded on actual research? For example, think about the number of times have you heard that multitasking can help you become more productive. In reality, research has found that trying to perform more than one task at the same time seriously impairs speed, accuracy and productivity.

So what lessons from psychology can you use to increase your productivity? Consider some of the following:

- ✓ Avoid multitasking when working on complex or dangerous tasks

- ✓ Focus on the task at hand

- ✓ Eliminate distractions

Be Healthier

Psychology can also be a useful tool for improving your overall health. From ways to encourage exercise and better nutrition to new treatments for depression, the field of health psychology offers a wealth of beneficial strategies that can help you to be healthier and happier.

Some examples that you can apply directly to your own life:

- ✓ Studies have shown that both sunlight and artificial light can reduce the symptoms of seasonal affective disorder

- ✓ Research has demonstrated that exercise can contribute to greater psychological well-being.

- ✓ Studies have found that helping people understand the risks of unhealthy behaviors can lead to healthier choices

PHSYCOLOGY AND HUMAN BEHAVIOR

Human behaviour is a curious thing. A range of factors, including our upbringing, what we've been taught, our culture, and our religious beliefs, influence the way we behave. It's also influenced by what we see happening around us and how effectively people encourage us to change our preconceived ideas.

Behaviour change marketing helps people assess what they believe by offering new insights into issues. It's not about coercing people into believing something new, but looking into an issue that's current or relevant. It can encourage them to think about issues that they would not normally take notice of.

You cannot force someone to think in a certain way, but by explaining issues around a topic, you can get a community talking and encourage change. Behaviour change marketing focuses on this innate need for people to discuss matters that affect them. Even matters that are being discussed by others can become important to someone who would normally not even think about an issue.

Take climate change. Because the topic has become

an issue that interests the general public, it is able to affect the way people act. People are now more likely to recycle, reduce and reuse, try to buy less or consume less, and to think about their habits. This topic has entered the public arena because people have been educated about what they can do to reduce climate change. Even people who do not change their behaviour have been encouraged to think about climate change as an issue.

Part of behaviour change marketing is to persuade or convince people of the need to change. This could be through promoting behaviour change as good or necessary. Sometimes the reasons people behave the way they do has less to do with their beliefs or any strongly held convictions and more to do with following trends. If people believe that others are conscientiously recycling, then they are more likely to do it themselves.

Other ways behaviour change marketing can work is to appeal to people's morality, to promote the costs or benefits of making a change, or to show that it is socially good to make a change. There are obvious moral and social issues with drink driving, for example, as you are potentially affecting others and not just yourself. Then there may be cost benefits to making a change: for example, buying ecologically friendly light bulbs may actually save you money.

As fantastically (and fanatically) self-aware organisms, we humans tend to ascribe great importance to our intellectual processes: We're rational and reasoning creatures, we assert, capable of stepping back and assessing our own behavior through an analytical lens.

Like any other biological entity, however, we're interacting with and responding to our environment in myriad ways well beyond the realm of our conscious perception. We usually take these subconscious, autonomic aspects of our being for granted, but naturally, they're fundamental to both our appreciation of the world around us and, critically, our day-to-day survival.

We don't need to compel ourselves to shiver when the mercury drops; our hand recoils at the lick of the flame or the bite of the dog. Thankfully, we don't have to think our way through the mechanics of walking in order to pull it off – start trying to, and you're liable to beeline for the pavement.

The conscious and the subconscious, the voluntary and the involuntary: When it comes to Homo sapiens, these processes aren't either-or propositions. They're thoroughly intertwined, influencing and echoing one another. In short, human beings (breaking news) are complicated systems, and the study of human behavior a complex task. Parsing out behavioral and emotional nuances requires zoomed-in looks at the tempos and intensities of all kinds of physical and psychological networks – and a holistic, big-picture perspective of how those networks interface with one another.

Understanding human behavior

The reason most people fail to understand human behaviour correctly is that they look at their behaviour without taking other variables into consideration.

If you had the goal of understanding a car's wheel, can you analyze the wheel alone without trying to understand its relationship with the other parts of the car?

If you did so then you might get the wheel incorrectly or fail to understand its function. For example you might never understand why the wheel has certain holes in the middle and even assume that its faulty but when you come to know that this wheel will fit into a rotating shaft then the holes in the center will make all the sense in the world.

The same goes for humans, You wont understand human behavior correctly before you take into consideration the person's beliefs, values, lifestyle, way of thinking and all other variables that affect him directly or indirectly.

A perfect real life example for understanding human behaviour

Brian,a self made millionaire, was a confident and charming person. Brian was so proud of himself and the main psychological identity he used to identify with was being a self made millionaire.

One day Brian discovered that he developed a weird obsessive compulsive disorder that forced him to check whether he left his car's door unlocked or not every few minutes!

For the first instance it might seem to a person who knows little about psychology that a problem happened with Brian's brain chemistry, which is a part of the truth, but he will never be able to guess what was going on unless he analyzes Brian's personality in more details.

In the past few weeks Brian has been seeing a recurring dream where his car gets stolen. Again to a person who knows little about the human nature it might seem that Brian is afraid to lose his car and that his fears were fed by this dream but that conclusion is wrong as well.

In the past couple of months Brian faced serious problems with his business that threatened its continuity and threatened his main and most important psychological identity. After all if he went out of business he wont be that self made millionaire anymore and he will lose his money.

Understanding Human nature by connecting the elements together

Because dreams always come in the form of symbols the loss of the car in Brian's dream was just a reflection of his fear of loss of his status. In other words the dream meant that Brian was concerned about losing his status or prestige! (see what does your dream mean)

Because the subconscious mind thinks using symbols and because logic is ignored to a certain extent during its operation Brian's mind forced him to develop that obsessive compulsive disorder because it was so concerned about the threat of the loss of his status.

In other words, Brian developed that disorder because he was too afraid to lose his status and checking whether the car was locked or not was a reflection of his fear of losing his car if he became poor.

This is how to understand human behaviour

When trying to understand human behaviour don't ever examine a single item without examining all the items in the system.

If a woman fears cats then instead of quickly assuming that a traumatic experience with cats happened to her when she was young you should try to look at other aspects of her life.

Could this fear of cats be a reflection of her fear of other women?

Could her low self esteem made her vulnerable to the presence of other women who were symbolized in the form of cats by her subconscious mind?

Of course i am not asking you to study the previous examples by hard then say that each man who develops such a disorder is afraid to lose his status or that each woman who fears cats has low self esteem but instead i am asking you to take a deeper look in order to understand the human behaviour perfectly.

Human behavior is very much inconsistent. In behavior, we aren't able to assume one pair blueprint of behavior. Levitt classified behavior as; (Id) triggered behavior, (ii) determined behavior, (iii) Goal-oriented behavior. From these observations, it may be known that behavior is a reliant element. By understanding behavior, an individual may predict, direct, transform and control behavior of group or individuals. There are generally four standard assumptions concerning character of folks: individual distinctions, a great person, caused behavior (motivation) and worthiness of the individual (human dignity).

11 Main Aspects of Human Behaviour

1.Psychology

Psychology is the science of human behaviour, Behaviour of an individual refers to anything an individual does.

An act of behaviour has three aspects:

Cognition-to become aware of or know something,

Affection-to have a certain feeling about it, and

Conation-to act in a particular way or direction after the feeling.

Human behaviour may be covert (expressed inside) or overt (expressed outside). While symbolic adoption is an example of covert behaviour, use adoption is an example of overt behaviour.

2. Personality

Personality is the unique, integrated and organized system of all behaviour of a person. Personality is the sum total of one's experience, thoughts and actions; it includes all behaviour patterns, traits and characteristics that make up a person. A person's physical traits, attitudes, habits and, emotional and psychological characteristics are all parts of one's personality.

Genetically influence on personality is seen clearly in the effect of physiology on physique and temperament, their interaction, and the role of nervous system in the acquisition of personality traits.

The cultural influence commences at birth with the infant's response to environment and continues throughout life as the influence of the home, community and society increases during growth and maturity of the individual. Parents, teachers and friends exercise great influence on the formation of attitudes and of the personality as a whole.

Sme commonly used personality types are introverts and extroverts. According to Guilford (1965), the introverts are people whose interests are turned inward upon themselves and their own thoughts, whereas the extroverts are those whose interests are turned outward upon the environment.

The introvert generally shuns social contacts and is inclined to be solitary, whereas the extrovert seeks social contacts and enjoys them. Lying in between are found people who are neither extrovert nor introvert, they are called ambiverts.

3. Interest

An interest is a preference for one activity over another. The selection and ranking of different activities along a like- dislike dimension is known as expressed interest. An interest is made manifest (visible), when a person voluntarily participates in an activity.

There is no necessary relationship between expressed interest and manifest interest, though in many situations they tend to coincide or overlap. Many individuals engage in some activities which they claim to dislike and just on the reverse, many people may refuse to engage in activities which they claim to enjoy.

4. Attitude

Allport (1935) defined attitude as a mental state of readiness, organized through experience, exerting a directive and dynamic influence upon the individual's response to all objects and situations with which it is related.

Attitudes have certain characteristics:

1. Attitudes are formed in relation to objects, persons and values. Attitudes are not innate, but are formed as a result of individual's contact with the environment.

2. Attitudes have direction; positive or favourable, negative or unfavourable. They also vary in degrees.

3. Attitudes are organized into a system and do not stand loosely or separately.

4. Attitudes are rooted in motivation and provide a meaningful background for individual's overt behaviour.

5. Attitudes develop through a consistency among responses. They are more stable and enduring than opinions.

6. Attitudes are prone to change. Changes in attitude

may be brought about by training and, other instructional methods and aids.

5. Emotions

Emotions denote a state of being moved, stirred up or aroused and involve impulses, feelings and physical and psychological reactions. A negative emotional response may lead to non-cooperation and non-participation in programmes, stoppage of work or even destruction of the work done. In a programme of planned change, the extension agent should take care of the state of emotion of the client system.

Guilford (1965) suggested the following rules for emotional control:

(i) Avoid emotion provoking situations,

(ii) Change the emotion provoking situation,

(iii) Increase skills for coping with the situation,

(iv) Re-interpret the situation,

(v) Keep working towards the goal,

(vi) Find substitute outlets, and

(vii) Develop a sense of humour.

6. Wishes

According to Chitambar (1997), a wish is a pattern of behaviour which involves:

(a) Anticipated future satisfaction,

(b) Which the person believes is reasonably likely of attainment, and

(c) Towards which the individual usually relates some of his/her present behaviour.

While wish-goals are oriented toward achievement in the future, what is significant is its influence on behaviour in the present. Wishes are based on subjective judgement which may at times be irrational and otherwise faulty. At any one time, a person may have several wishes and it may become necessary to set priorities for their achievement.

7. Prejudice

PREJUDICE means pre-judgement. Judgement before due examination and consideration of facts, and based on certain assumptions generally lead to the formation of prejudice. Prejudice is normally negative and difficult to reverse. Prejudices may lead to hostile attitude towards persons or objects. Expressing ill feeling or hostility towards some minority or caste groups, or an innovation are examples of prejudice.

An effort in reducing prejudice must start with the understanding about its origin. Personal contact, use of mass media, suitable enactments having penal provision, economic changes resulting in greater security etc. may help in reducing prejudice.

8. Stereotype

Stereotypes are fixed images formed in one's mind about people, practices or various other social phenomena on the basis of experience, attitudes, values, impressions or without any direct experience, Stereotypes help in knowing how people perceive various groups of people or practice or various other social phenomena.

Stereotypes have certain characteristics:

Uniformity-members belonging to a particular group share the stereotype.

Direction-may be positive or negative.

Intensity-indicates strength of the stereotype.

Quality-refers to content, the kind of image provided by the stereotype.

9. Thinking and Reasoning

According to Garrett (1975), thinking is behaviour which is often implicit and hidden, and in which symbols (images, ideas, and concepts) are ordinarily employed. Group thinking, in which a number of persons participate in the solution of a problem, is usually more efficient than individual effort and is often more satisfactory.

In reasoning, the thinking process is applied to the solution of problems. There are, in general, two methods of solving problems-deductive and inductive. Deductive reasoning starts with a general fact or proposition, under which various specific items can be placed or classified.

Inductive reasoning, on the other hand, starts with observations and proceeds step by step to a general conclusion. Both methods are employed in most learning situations.

10. Frustration and Adjustment

A common pattern of human behaviour involves hopes for future achievement. Such ambitions and goals are generally termed as wish. Frustration is a condition in which an individual perceives the wish goal blocked or unattainable. This creates some tension in the individual. When faced with such a situation, the individual tries to make several kinds of adjustments in the behaviour pattern. This is achieved through defense mechanism.

A defense mechanism is a device, a way of behaving, that a person uses unconsciously to protect oneself from ego-involving frustrations. This helps the individual to reduce tension. Following Chitambar (1990) and Krech and Crutchfield (1984) some adjustment patterns i.e. defense mechanisms are presented in brief.

Rationalization occurs when a person unconsciously explains the situation to oneself by reasoning that, after all the individual never did really wish to achieve the goal. Example, 'grapes are sour'. Rationalization differs from alibis and excuses in that the first one is unconscious in nature, while the latter two are conscious.

Rationalization makes an individual feel comfortable by helping avoid unpalatable situations by justifying one's own behaviour in conformity with the existing social practices and values. Hence, rationalization functions as one of the major obstacles to change.

Aggression is caused by frustration of dominant motives. Aggression may be turned outwards i.e.

directed towards other persons, or directed inwards i.e. makes oneself responsible for whatever has happened, or may be repressed without any overt expression.

Aggression may be expressed in the form of anger, actual physical violence against objects and people, verbal attacks and fantasies of violence.

Identification is a common form of adjustment in which the individual lives through the achievement of others, participating vicariously (as a substitute) in their success. Parents could receive genuine satisfaction from their children's success, which they themselves could not achieve.

Projection means transferring one's emotion and ascribing the source of emotion to another object. Projection is a tendency to 'push out' upon another person, one's own unrealized frustrated ambitions, or to attribute to another one's own faults.

Projection may take two forms-(i) in order to escape from facing the reality that a person has failed, the individual may blame another or even a non-existent person or factor. In another type, (ii) the individual reasons that one's own faults are also found in others to an even greater degree.

Fantasy or Day dreaming is a common form of adjustment to frustration. The individual enters an imaginary world in which the person's all wish goals are realized. Compensation is a reaction to a feeling of inferiority. The inferiority feeling may be based on real or imaginary deficiency, which may be physical or otherwise, and compensation is an attempt to overcome or neutralize the deficiency.

Compensation may take two forms:

(i) Substitution-when a new goal is substituted for a goal which is blocked and

(ii) Sublimation-when the substitution involves moral consideration i.e. changing a particular emotion in a socially valued and socially acceptable way. An individual may work hard and try to shine out to compensate for one's own deficiencies.

Regression means going back to a less mature level of behaviour. In certain frustrating situation, the behaviour of the individual tends to become primitive. The actions become less mature, more childish; the sensitivity of discriminations and judgements diminishes; feelings and emotions become more poorly differentiated and controlled, like those of a child. Example, a farmer dissatisfied with an innovation, may discontinue it and revert to the previous practice which may be old and uneconomic.

Repression is the mechanism by which wishes are not allowed to come out of the unconscious or thrown down into the unconscious. For example, a sex relationship not sanctioned by the society is generally repressed and gradually forgotten.

11. Deviant Behaviour

Some individuals' personality traits and behaviour differ considerably more than others' from the norms. Such behaviour is termed as deviant behaviour and the individuals are known as deviants.

Three essential aspects of deviant behaviour are presented, following Chitambar (1997):

1. Deviation is culturally defined. The same behaviour considered as deviant in one culture, may be regarded as normal or highly valued in another culture.

2. Deviation develops through the process of socialization, in the same way as normal behaviour does.

3. Deviation is a matter of degree. If the personality

traits and behaviour of individuals in a society are placed on a continuum, the majority would be near the centre, which would represent the area of accepted social norms. Outside this, will lie those individuals referred to as social deviants.

On one side-the 'high side'-will be those social deviants whose deviancy not only is approved by society, but also secures for them status, high recognition and praise. These 'desirable' deviants can bring about rapid social change.

On the other side, lie those deviants who by virtue of the extreme difference of their personality traits and behaviour are conspicuously set apart and disapproved by the society. They are considered as 'undesirable' deviants.

PSYCHOLOGY AND MINDSET

The media these days has sure created a whole lot of hype about "mindset?" So I'm officially giving my two cents of what mindset development is, and how you can actually change it. You can because there really is a psychology to mindset. Wouldn't you like to know what it is? Just do a search in your favorite Web browser for the word "Mindset." You'll get thousands of searches, but you'll also be hard-pressed to find one source online that understands how mindset works. Some might, sure. But with so many gurus and experts claiming to be able to help you evolve just by changing one (not so) teeny thing, wouldn't it be useful to know the truth? The truth about the psychology BEHIND the curtain of mindset? I think so too! So here it is. Mindset is really just about mind-shift. It's about the way you see the world. Think of mindset as the pair of lenses you choose to look through at the world.

You can wear rosy or gray. The truth is, your consistent thoughts only add to the positive, or negative, outlook of your life. This is what they mean by "self-fulfilling prophecy." Those media gurus and I agree that you must change your mindset to have the happiness you want. But it's simply NOT ENOUGH for me to tell you to simply "change your mindset" and wait for the magic happen. That's like me saying, "I'll drop a little fairy dust on your head, and your mind will instantly be cleared of all the goo." Sorry, mindset change doesn't work that way. No wonder so many frustrated humans are scurrying about in our society, looking for the NEXT guru that can answer, "How can you make me happy?" Wait no more. I can answer that question. The truth about mindset change is that it's so easy, you might wonder if fairy dust is involved. And you might wonder why you spent thousands of hours paying someone to help you be happy when I'm giving it to you for free. (You're welcome!) I'm going to describe something I call the "Mind Tree." Draw this out on a piece of paper as I explain it so it makes more sense. The trunk of your tree is a simple formula: thoughts create emotions; emotions create actions. Then two main branches spawn from thoughts: conscious and subconscious.

Those are the two types of thoughts--the first you can easily tap into and are aware of and the second you can't easily access. These subconscious thoughts lurk in the background of your mind. Your habitual thoughts are your mindset. These are the thoughts you have to change if you want to change your mindset. But here's the kicker: Your conscious thoughts make up only about 15% of your total thoughts, maybe less! Your subconscious thoughts make up the other 85%. Draw this on your mindset tree. Let it sink in. That means in order to change your mindset, you have to tap into those thoughts you don't even know you're thinking. Bad news, right? Well, not so fast. You can change your subconscious programming. There are so many ways, and that's where a GOOD guru comes in! From my pre-frontal cortex to yours (that's where your conscious thoughts are stored), here are just a few to get you started: First, identify what subconscious thoughts are ones that are no longer serving you well. They may sound something like this: "I am never good enough. Money doesn't grow on trees and doesn't come easy. Hard work is the only work that pays, etc." You can see how just one subconscious thought can create a whole heap of trouble, can't you? Second, choose to change.

Oh, yes, you know I had to say it. CHOOSE to change! The reality is, most people figure out what subconscious thoughts are actually holding them back but then won't do anything about it. Making the decision to take action is a very big step. And it's vital. (The reasons for not taking action are a whole therapy session in itself, so we'll save that for another time!) Three, implement tools. Create new habitual thoughts, affirm what is truth, post sticky notes all over your house and in your car, use EFT, journal ad nauseum, use a "change buddy" for motivation, have lucid dreams, talk about your change efforts until you are sick, and keep moving in THAT direction, not the OTHER direction. You have so many ways to change your negative subconscious programming. One popular phrase is "Just Do It!" But what happens when "Just Do It" doesn't work? No, it's not a matter of willpower or strength. And it's not an issue of character. It's about sticktoitiveness, practice, and consistent follow-through. Yes, there is a psychology to mindset. Can you call it a day just by knowing that? No, but once you face those negative subconscious thoughts, you can shout from the rooftop "JOB DONE!"

A mindset is a belief that orients the way we handle situations — the way we sort out what is going on and what we should do. Our mindsets help us spot opportunities but they can trap us in self-defeating cycles.

This essay isn't about all the beliefs we might hold. It is about the beliefs that make a difference in our lives — the beliefs that distinguish people who are successful at what they do versus those who continually struggle.

THE STANFORD UNIVERSITY PSYCHOLOGIST CAROL DWECK (2006) POPULARIZED THE IDEA OF MINDSETS BY CONTRASTING DIFFERENT BELIEFS ABOUT WHERE OUR ABILITIES COME FROM.

If we have a fixed mindset that our ability is innate then a failure can be unsettling because it makes us doubt how good we are. In contrast, if we have a growth mindset then we expect that we can improve our ability — and a failure shows us what we need to work on. People with a fixed mindset are out to prove themselves, and get very defensive when someone suggests they made a mistake — they measure themselves by their failures. People with a growth mindset often show perseverance and resilience when they've committed errors — they become more motivated to work harder. You can imagine how much this fixed vs growth mindset can affect our lives.

My investigation of the nature of insight turned up a major difference between people (and organizations) who concentrate on ways to reduce errors versus others who, in addition to worrying about errors, are also excited about chances to make discoveries. The preoccupation with errors — the belief that the only way to improve performance is by reducing errors — seems to fit the fixed mindset, and the interest in discoveries — the belief that performance improvements depend both on cutting errors and on making insights — maps onto the growth mindset.

Other types of mindset can also make a big difference.

A few years ago my wife Helen and I studied police officers, soldiers and marines who had shown outstanding skills in dealing with civilians. We wanted to see what set them apart from colleagues who typically intimidated civilians in order to get them to comply. We discovered that these "Good Strangers" (as they were called) shared one trait — they all had a mindset that their colleagues didn't. Sure, they worried about their own safety, and that of their buddies. Sure, they wanted to achieve the mission, and to follow the rules. But in addition, the Good Strangers sought to gain the trust of civilians. One police officer explained to us that in every encounter with civilians, even when he was arresting a lawbreaker, he tried to conduct himself so that the civilian trusted him more at the end of the encounter than the beginning. He believed that being a professional meant doing his job in a way that fostered trust. Think back to your encounters with police — I suspect some of these encounters did not increase your trust in the officer.

We found a fourth important mindset in our work with police and military. Many of them believed that the way to get someone to do what you want is to command obedience, through intimidation or in other ways. But the Good Strangers believed that they often could get cooperation voluntarily. It took skill and took more time but it had a long-term payoff. And it built trust.

Mindsets aren't just any beliefs. They are beliefs that orient our reactions and tendencies. They serve a number of cognitive functions. They let us frame situations: they direct our attention to the most important cues, so that we're not overwhelmed with information. They suggest sensible goals so that we know what we should be trying to achieve. They prime us with reasonable courses of action so that we don't have to puzzle out what to do. When our mindsets become habitual, they define who we are, and who we can become.

We've looked at four mindsets that distinguish people who are doomed to struggle versus those who can be successful: a) fixed/growth, b) preoccupation with failure versus eagerness for discoveries, c) wanting to build trust, and d) seeking voluntary cooperation. Here is a fifth mindset that emerged from a project my research team did with Child Protective Services caseworkers. The mediocre caseworkers believed that their job was to follow procedures, but the best caseworkers saw the job as continually solving problems.

We found this same following procedures/solving problems contrast in other groups such as nurses and petrochemical plant operators. We also found it in another study of police officers. Recent academy graduates tried to add to their playbook, believing that if they learned enough procedures they could do the job. In contrast, the seasoned police officers appreciated that there were never enough procedures, and they had to be ready to solve unique problems. In fact, some of the seasoned police officers got a little bored when everything went too smoothly. They appreciated a good challenge — obviously they had a growth mindset.

The wrong mindsets can get in our way. A fixed mindset about our ability will inhibit our progress. So will a procedural mindset, governed by the belief that adding more plays in our playbook will turn us into experts. A mindset to eliminate mistakes will stifle our curiosity. A mindset about dominating civilians will damage a police officer's interactions with civilians and will result in more physical fights and reduced safety.

One of the most powerful aspects of mindsets is how quickly they can be shifted, and how powerful the consequences can be. Unlike skills that have to be practiced again and again, mindsets sometimes show dramatic shifts. Reading Dweck's book Mindset for an hour or two is enough to alter our beliefs about our abilities and motivate us to change to the growth mindset. In my work with police officers I heard many stories of officers who expected to demand obedience until they saw a supervisor speaking quietly and getting compliance.

One police officer remembered an event, decades earlier, at the beginning of his career. It was a dark night in a dangerous neighborhood. He and his supervisor, Raymond, had spotted a suspect and were closing in to make the arrest. On the way, they passed a mildly inebriated homeless man, sitting on a stoop, and the man whispered, "He's got a gun, Raymond." Sure enough, the suspect was armed and they were able to make the arrest safely. Afterwards, he asked his supervisor why the vagrant had warned them. Raymond explained that the man was harmless and he had tried to look out for him and get him to shelters when necessary. And in that instant, the rookie officer decided he wanted to have that kind of Good Stranger relationship with the people in the community. He wanted them to trust him and look out for him, rather than fear him.

Of course, it doesn't always go this easily — some of the police and military I encountered were just too determined to take no unnecessary risks. And I suspect some of the people Dweck has encountered couldn't let go of their fear of failures. But others are able to shift their beliefs and mindsets. Dweck tells the story of Jimmy, a junior high school student who had shown little interest in his classes. Then he sat through a session describing the growth mindset and tearfully asked, "You mean I don't have to be dumb?" From that point, Jimmy became a hard-working student. Mindsets are powerful, and shifting them can be sudden and transformative.

UNDERSTANDING HOW YOUR MIND WORKS

Our brains perform so many functions that living with one can sometimes become a confusing mess. How many times have you had mixed thoughts, feelings, ideas, solutions, and memories clammoring for some mental real estate, all while trying to stay focused on something else?

Cognitive psychologists have tried to make sense out of this for many years, but most of their output has been impractical. However, over the past 20 years a major theme emerged that was a breakthrough, which isn't something new to regular Psychology Today readers. The key finding was that our brains have two major types of processes: those that operate automatically (usually called System 1) and those that are more effortful (System 2). The research that demonstrated this won Daniel Kahneman the Nobel Prize.

I found this rough distinction to be somewhat helpful for my counseling clients, but it has been difficult to translate it into useful tools. So I have been working to find a better application for therapy, and recently arrived at what I call the Three Frames of Mind. All three have a purpose, none of them are superior to any other, and there are variations on each. Readers familiar with Kahneman's research will notice that the first two Frames, (Engaged & Automatic) are both forms of System 1 and the other (Analytic) is a practical way of looking at System 2.

Frames of Mind

For the descriptions below to make sense, I invite you to think of a great example for each one from your own life. You may have even used all 3 in the past couple of minutes reading this book. Once you get a good sense of them, they should become more obvious and easy to work with. I will also provide an example of each that happened to me recently hanging out with a friend.

1. Engaged Mind: this is the state of being totally immersed in, or connected to, what we are doing in the present moment. When we are fully present in a conversation, skiing down a mountain, crying after hearing about a friend having cancer, or taking the first bite of the best slice of pizza in the world; basically when our thoughts and attention are fully connected to what is happening here-and-now, that is Engaged Mind. People that are able to Engage in their daily activities (rather than zoning out or being distracted by other thoughts), are generally happier

and more satisfied with their lives and relationships. Recent research even shows that being in Engaged mind reduces base levels of the stress hormone cortisol.

Being Engaged doesn't mean an absence of pain, since what might be happening at any given moment could be physically or emotionally painful. It just means being connected to whatever is going on. Current counseling approaches based on mindfulness are designed to help people improve their experience of Engagement, and this is often one of the goals my clients have in therapy. You can read my post on Mindfulness here: An Introduction to Mindfulness.

Example: When I am hanging out with my friend I am totally caught up in listening to a story and then telling one of my own. I feel connected and the interactions are spontaneous and free of impression management. I am fully present in each moment, unconcerned with anything else that is happening outside of that conversation. Time flies by.

2. Automatic Mind: our brain is constantly conducting an enormous range tasks. For example, we become aware of any changes in the environment (new sounds, changes in light or temperature, quick movements, etc) and any pains or bodily sensations

that deserve to be noticed (and some that don't). We effortlessly make evaluations and judgments about things being positive or negative (including ourselves), categorize our experiences, and make decisions about things we need to do and have to remember. We have scenes from our past triggered and have feelings and sensations about things that might occur in the future. We form habits to Automate major parts of our lives, and are pulled out of moments with memories or questions. This non-stop flow of information is part of being human, and we spend a large percentage of our lives swimming in this stream. This is Automatic Mind.

The content of Automatic Mind is determined by current internal and environmental conditions, instincts, perceptions, and prior learning. The flow is essential for our survival and helps us adapt among countless other things, but it is also full of misinformation, distortions, and biases. Although they can be beneficial, the immediate judgments and impulses, engrained habits, and intense moods that Automatically grip us are usually the source of our greatest problems and pain, especially when it becomes routine. If Automatic thoughts and feelings are pleasant, then spending a lot of time in this frame is great! But when those things are more negative or troubling, or are so strong that we can't stay Engaged, then Automatic Mind can become an unbearable place that we try to escape from. Most people come to counseling for things related to Automatic Mind.

Example: During a slow moment of the conversation with my friend, my mind wanders to what I am doing after we part. I mentally run through a list of things to get at the grocery store, and also replay an argument I got into with someone else a few hours earlier that makes me get a bit anxious. I am not completely present in what is happening here-and-now, but am off and running with this Automatic flow, losing track of the details of the conversation in the process, and feeling anxious.

3. Analytic Mind: since we are self-aware creatures, we have the ability to intentionally step back from our current thoughts, feelings, and experiences to observe them, manipulate information in our minds, and solve problems. All of the complex reasoning we can do is what I call Analytic Mind.

Since there are so many different ways Analytic Mind can work, I offer 6 broad categories below. Also, many of these thought processes also take place in Automatic Mind. The difference here is that Analytic Mind is when we intentionally choose to use these abilities.

-Observe: we can observe other people, as well as the workings or our own minds.

-Reflect: we can replay events in our memories, and arrive at new perspectives.

-Solve: we can take immediate issues and problems and find solutions or understanding.

-Plan: we can plan deep into the future and create backup options.

-Focus: we can sustain attention on something important

-Imagine: we can use our imaginations to run through how something may play out.

Most of our complex reasoning skills come online at the beginning of adolescence and develop into adulthood. When we make decisions after Analyzing a situation, we are less likely to make mistakes or have biased perspectives. Other problems can arise here when we stay in this frame too much by "over-Analyzing" things, develop a rigidity of thinking, or don't use it enough! Our Analytic Minds also come into conflict with Automatically generated emotions and intuition, which can leave us in a states of confusion, indecision, or "cognitive dissonance." You can read more about that here: Resolving Cognitive Dissonance.

Example: After noticing my anxiety, I decided to try and re-Engage in the conversation. However, I stayed anxious and kept having difficulty being involved. I decided to take a couple minutes to take a closer look at my anxiety to understand why it was so strong, and to reason through it. I reflected on the earlier argument, and realized that I made a critical mistake, and I then focused on developing a plan of how to apologize and make things right again. After doing this, I was able to Engage again with my friend.

Mastering Your Mind

You may think your success is determined by your intelligence, experience, environment, or even your personality. But research suggests that it's your point of view – your mindset – that may be the key.

The mindset you adopt for yourself profoundly affects the way you lead your life, says Carol Dweck, PhD, author of Mindset: The New Psychology of Success.

Your mindset -- the difference in how you react to feedback or accomplishment -- can affect your performance in school, relationships, business and even parenting.

Dweck's research suggests there are just two different mindsets: fixed and growth. Those with a fixed mindset need to keep proving themselves over and over, while those with a growth mindset believe their basic qualities can be cultivated through their own efforts.

What type of mindset do you have?

Here's one quick way to find out: Think back to your school days. If you got a bad grade in school, would you often give up, saying the class was just a waste of time, or would you tend to tell yourself you just needed to study harder?

If you were likely to give up, you are likely to have a fixed mindset; if you decided to work harder, you probably have a growth mindset.

Someone with a fixed mindset is typically quick to interpret disappointments as utter failure. "Nothing ventured, nothing lost," becomes their philosophy, as they get increasingly reluctant to attempt new things and believe in themselves. They're also likely to under- or over-estimate their abilities, setting themselves up for frustration and failure.

On the other hand, those with a growth mindset tend to be quick to create a simple strategy to deal with problems as they occur. And they're better able to accurately identify their own strengths and weaknesses.

Interestingly, Dweck says that research done in the brain-wave lab at Columbia University, in New York, shows a link between actual brain activity and one's perspective.

In the study, participants with both types of mindsets were asked hard questions. When they got feedback, those with a fixed mindset were only interested in how well they scored, and didn't want to learn the right answer. Those with a growth mindset listened to information that would enhance their knowledge, and seemed less focused on how they did on the questions themselves.

The good news is that you can actually change your mindset. But there are some things Dweck says you should know:

Your mindset is part of your make-up. Understanding your mindset can help you think and react in a different way.

If you have a fixed mindset, everything is about

outcome: getting the grade, or rising to the top of the organization, for example. If you have a growth mindset, it's about valuing what you do regardless of the outcomes.

Generally, those with a fixed mindset prefer effortless success. It helps them prove their talent.

You're not always in your dominant mindset. Many people have elements of both mindsets, and you can have different mindsets in different areas of your life. For example, you might think your artistic ability is fixed ("I just can't draw") but you hope to develop athletic ability by taking golf lessons. Whatever mindset people have in a particular area will guide them in that realm.

If you have a growth mindset, you most likely believe that abilities can be cultivated. But you should know some things probably can't be cultivated, such as preferences or values.

People with fixed mindsets have just as much confidence as those with growth mindsets. But someone with a fixed mindset tends to be more fragile and susceptible to setbacks.

Those with growth mindsets don't always feel confident. In fact, they sometimes plunge into something just because they're not good at it. They just want to try.

If you want to re-adjust your mindset, how do you do it? Start by catching yourself giving up when something starts to get difficult -- say when you're doing a crossword puzzle, or playing video game or a sport. "Put yourself in a growth mindset. Picture your brain forming new connections as you meet the challenge and learn. Keep on going," Dweck suggests.

She also encourages people to leave their comfort zones and seek constructive criticism. "We can choose partners, make friends, hire people who make us feel faultless. But think about it – do you want to never grow?"

Why You Need To Develop A Growth Mindset

"If you imagine less, less will be what you undoubtedly deserve." ~ Debbie Millman

It is said that you have a growth mindset if you are one of those people who believe that—by investing enough time, effort and study—you will be able to acquire any ability. If you believe abilities are innate and that, simply, there is no way of doing that for what you were not born, then you have a fixed mindset.

Those with a fixed mindset are very afraid of failure because they see it as a sign of weakness or lack of ability in a given field. People with a growth mindset don't care much about failure because they know that they can learn from it and therefore improve their performance.

Carol Dweck, Ph.D. in Psychology and professor at Standford University, has studied how these types of mindsets influence peoples' lives. She has concluded that people with growth mentality are more successful in every aspect of their lives and live with lower stress levels (you can read the outcome of her research in her book of 2006, Mindset: The New Psychology of Success).

Someone with a fixed mindset sees effort as something unnecessary. They will tend to avoid challenges, surrender when obstacles appear, ignore criticisms and feel threaten with someone else's success. As a consequence, they will become stagnant and will never reach their potential.

Someone with a growth mindset perceives effort as the necessary path to mastery. They will accept challenges despite the risk, fight against adversities, learn from criticisms and find inspiration in someone else's success.

Good news is that it's possible to work on a fixed mindset and transform it into a growth one. The best way to achieve this is through deliberate practice. You have to take active part, and take some steps which are against your beliefs. It's your daily actions the ones that change the perception of yourself.

For example, if you have given up doing sports because you think it's not your thing, try to run only one kilometer at a pace you feel comfortable with. Do it again another day, and another... and another. In a few days you will be easily running two kilometers and in some weeks, five. As months go by you will see that you can even increase your speed little by little and achieve decent times. Contrary to what you believe, your identity could end up including the word "athlete".

If you think that "being organized" is not for you and that you are a natural procrastinator, then you are limiting very much your personal development and you'll waste a good part of your life just by not trying to improve. Start by practicing the steps that will make you more productive. Concentrate on the process, not on the final outcome (it will come later), and the transformation will happen.

HOW TO USE PSYCHOLOGY TO BATTLE PROCRASTINATION

I have read a lot about procrastination (mainly because I've done it all my life), and found many different reported causes. But it all boils down to the age-old battle of pleasure versus pain. It is said that all human behavior falls into two categories: acquiring pleasure or avoiding pain. Our decisions and actions are really efforts to either gain pleasurable feelings or avoid some sort of pain or uncomfortable feeling.

So how does this relate to procrastination? Procrastinators are focused on doing activities that are pleasurable while avoiding activities that have perceived pain.

Watching TV, playing video games, reading, and napping are all activities that can be more pleasurable than working. These may be obvious but work-related tasks can also reinforce delay. Tasks such as checking email, looking at website stats, doing research, and training are all ways that we can feel busy without really getting anything accomplished. Sometimes it's more fun to learn about how to do things than actually doing them.

For some, the pain is the discomfort of the work

needed to complete their task. These people look at what the job requires and want to avoid the process. It can also be that many procrastinators tie their self-worth with their performance and the fear of being criticized for their work overcomes the need to complete it.

Many strive for perfectionism, but their fear of failure motivates them to avoid the task altogether. The perceived pain of making a mistake, being criticized, or letting someone else down can be too much to bear. There is more to procrastination than just being lazy.

Procrastination is one of the biggest obstacles to productivity and a guilty refuge of creatives everywhere. It's something we're all guilty of, and something we all have our own tactics (with varying degrees of success) to combat. What makes us procrastinate? Why is the temptation so great, even when we know we need to complete the task at hand? First, let's look at the psychology of procrastination.

While everyone procrastinates to some extent, not everyone is a chronic procrastinator. There are relatively harmless instances of procrastination—not starting a project until you've gone to the washroom, checked Facebook, refilled your coffee and organized everything in your top desk drawer, or leaving your least favourite task for Friday afternoon. But there are also the unhealthy procrastination habits that find you staring at a blank computer screen for an hour, or that leave you awake in the middle of the night in a cold sweat, agonizing over the work you didn't complete, wondering how you'll ever get it done the next day.

Understand Procrastination

There are a lot of misconceptions about what causes procrastination. For many years, I felt that procrastination meant that I was lazy and unfocused. Whether it was a university paper due or a client presentation I had to have ready at 9 am, I'd find myself awake in the middle of the night skimming articles on the Battle of the Bulge or the care and feeding of chinchillas (I've never had a chinchilla) while sweating about all the work I hadn't done. Conventional wisdom denotes the source of procrastination to be a lack of willpower or poor time management, and so that was what I believed my problem to be.

However, in more recent studies psychologists have understood procrastination to be closely related to our emotional brain—a coping mechanism driven by our own fear of failure. By avoiding tasks that are intimidating and overwhelming, and focusing on something less stressful, we give our brain temporary relief. Unfortunately, as all procrastinators know, the end result is usually the last-minute rush to complete projects, coupled with intensified anxiety, a lack of sleep, and reduced quality of work.

Once we understand that procrastination is mostly fear and anxiety based, we can learn more meaningful methods to overcome it. The age-old "just get started!" advice doesn't fit as neatly into the narrative of procrastination when we are aware that most people are avoiding things they are anxious about.

"It really has nothing to do with time-management," says Association for Psychological Science Fellow Joseph Ferrari, a professor of psychology at DePaul University. "To tell the chronic procrastinator to just do it would be like saying to a clinically depressed person, cheer up."

Why Do We Procrastinate and Wait Until the Last Minute?

We all procrastinate at some time or another, and researchers suggest that the problem can be particularly pronounced among students. An estimated 25 to 75 percent of college students procrastinate on academic work.

One 2007 study found that a whopping 80 to 95 percent of college students procrastinated on a regular basis, particularly when it came to completing assignments and coursework. A 1997 survey found that procrastination was one of the top reasons why Ph.D. candidates failed to complete their dissertations.

According to Ferrari, Johnson, and McCown, there are some major cognitive distortions that lead to academic procrastination.

Students tend to:

Overestimate how much time they have left to perform tasks

Overestimate how motivated they will be in the future

Underestimate how long certain activities will take to complete

Mistakenly assume that they need to be in the right frame of mind to work on a project

As you read through that list, you can probably recall a few times in the past that the same sort of logic has led you to put things off until later. Remember that time that you thought you had a week left to finish a project that was really due the next day? How about the time you decided not to clean up your apartment because you "didn't feel like doing it right now."

We often assume that projects won't take as long to finish as they really will, which can lead to a false sense of security when we believe that we still have plenty of time to complete these tasks. One of the biggest factors contributing to procrastination is the notion that we have to feel inspired or motivated to work on a task at a particular moment.

The reality is that if you wait until you're in the right frame of mind to do certain tasks (especially undesirable ones), you will probably find that the right time simply never comes along and the task never gets completed.

Self-doubt can also play a major role. When you are unsure of how to tackle a project or insecure in your abilities, you might find yourself putting it off in favor of working on other tasks.

The Negative Impact Of Procrastination

It's not just students who fall into the "I'll do it later" trap. According to Joseph Ferrari, a professor of psychology at DePaul University in Chicago and author of Still Procrastinating: The No Regret Guide to Getting It Done, around 20 percent of U.S. adults are chronic procrastinators.

These people don't just procrastinate occasionally; it's a major part of their lifestyle. They pay their bills late, don't start work on big projects until the night before the deadline, delay holiday shopping until Christmas Eve, and even file their income tax returns late.

Unfortunately, this procrastination can have a serious impact on a number of life areas, including a person's mental health. In a 2007 study, researchers found that at the beginning of the semester, students who were procrastinators reported less illness and lower stress levels than non-procrastinators. This changed dramatically by the end of the term when procrastinators reported higher levels of stress and illness.

Not only can procrastination have a negative impact on your health; it can also harm your social relationships. By putting things off, you are placing a burden on the people around you. If you habitually turn in projects late or dawdle until the last minute, the people who depend on you such as your friends, family, co-workers, and fellow students can become resentful.

The Reasons Why We Procrastinate

In addition to the reasons why we procrastinate, we often come up with a number of excuses or rationalizations to justify our behavior.

According to Tuckman, Abry, and Smith, there are 15 key reasons why people procrastinate:

- ✓ Not knowing what needs to be done

- ✓ Not knowing how to do something

- ✓ Not wanting to do something

- ✓ Not caring if it gets done or not

- ✓ Not caring when something gets done

- ✓ Not feeling in the mood to do it

- ✓ Being in the habit of waiting until the last minute

- ✓ Believing that you work better under pressure

- ✓ Thinking that you can finish it at the last minute

- ✓ Lacking the initiative to get started

- ✓ Forgetting

- ✓ Blaming sickness or poor health

- ✓ Waiting for the right moment

- ✓ Needing time to think about the task

- ✓ Delaying one task in favor of working on another

How Do Procrastinators Differ From Non-Procrastinators?

In most cases, procrastination is not a sign of a serious problem. It's a common tendency that we all give in to at some point or another. It is only in cases where procrastination becomes so chronic that it begins to have a serious impact on a person's daily life that it becomes a more serious issue. In such instances, it's not just a matter of having poor time management skills; it's an indication of what Ferrari refers to as a maladaptive lifestyle.

"Non-procrastinators focus on the task that needs to be done. They have a stronger personal identity and are less concerned about what psychologists call 'social esteem'—how others like us—as opposed to self-esteem which is how we feel about ourselves," explained Dr. Ferrari in an interview with the American Psychological Association.

According to psychologist Piers Steel, people who don't procrastinate tend to be high in the personality trait known as conscientiousness, one of the broad dispositions identified by the big 5 theory of personality. People who are high in conscientiousness also tend to be high in other areas including self-discipline, persistence, and personal responsibility.

Falling prey to these cognitive distortions is easy, but fortunately, there are a number of different things you can do to fight procrastination and start getting things done on time.

HOW TO USE PSYCHOLOGY TO BOOST YOUR CONFIDENCE

Society offers us plenty of advice on how to be confident. "Just be yourself." "Fake it til you make it." "Dress for success." Tips fly at us from every direction, from mothers to magazine covers. Some of this advice can be useful, but it can ultimately feel ineffective or empty when we don't really believe in ourselves. We all battle core feelings about ourselves that can be negative and demoralizing. In response, we may find ourselves either sinking into self-shame or trying to build up our ego just to get through the day.

To truly construct a solid foundation of self-confidence, we have to dig a little deeper. There are many positive, psychological steps we can take to feel good about ourselves. Most importantly, we have to do two things: 1. Challenge the inner critic we all possess and 2. Practice self-compassion. With these goals in mind, we can start to take practical actions to feel more comfortable in our skin. Here are some powerful tools that can help us all feel more self-possessed.

How To Be Confident: Practice Self-Compassion

It's valuable to move through life with what mindfulness expert and interpersonal neurobiologist Dr. Daniel Siegel calls a COAL attitude, in which we are Curious, Open, Accepting, and Loving toward ourselves no matter what we're going through. That way, even if we feel humiliated and defeated, or our self-confidence has taken a hit, we won't waste time beating ourselves up. Instead, we learn from our experiences. Enhancing our self-compassion is an adaptive process that allows us to feel more self-acceptance, while simultaneously making real efforts to develop, both which help to establish our confidence.

Groundbreaking research by Dr. Kristin Neff has shown that self-compassion can actually be more valuable and adaptive than self-esteem. For instance, compared to self-esteem, self-compassion was associated with "greater emotional resilience, more accurate self-concepts, more caring relationship behavior, [and] less narcissism." When wondering how to be confident, practicing self-compassion is a great place to start. To fully understand why self-compassion is so crucial to our confidence, it's helpful to break down the three elements of self-compassion as defined by Neff.

Self-kindness vs Self-judgment – When we get carried away with judging and evaluating ourselves, our confidence tends to plummet. Imagine berating yourself before a date or a job interview. "You're not dressed right." "You're gonna be so awkward." These thoughts will likely increase our anxiety and even impair our ability to act natural and be ourselves. Now, imagine being kind to yourself instead, as if a friend is sitting beside you, offering encouragement and warmth. This "friend" doesn't have to build us up or offer false praise. It can simply say, "It's okay that you're nervous, but there's absolutely nothing wrong with you. I'm proud that you showed up and are trying this." While self-esteem is still often based on evaluation, self-compassion comes from having a kind attitude toward ourselves no matter what we're going through or taking on.

Mindfulness vs Over-identification with thoughts – Because our thoughts can go so negative at times, it's helpful to practice mindfulness as a way to avoid being consumed by this negativity. Mindfulness is a way of focusing our attention and accepting our thoughts and feelings without judgment, while also letting them go. Think about how athletes or performers have to actively focus on clearing their minds before they march onto the field or step out on the stage. It's hard to feel self-possessed and capable when our hearts are racing and heads are spinning with doubt and self-criticism. Whether through meditation or breathing exercises, mindfulness allows us to stay in our bodies in the moment and allow our thoughts to pass like cars on a train. We can notice and acknowledge them, but we don't board the train and get swept away. By not over-identifying with our negative or self-critical thoughts, we learn to live more in the moment and feel more self-possessed, both which can be key to feeling confident.

Common humanity vs Isolation – In her examination, Neff found that it's much easier to have self-compassion when we accept that we are all part of a shared human experience. In other words, we all make mistakes, and we all suffer. It's easy to attack ourselves when we view ourselves as different or alone in our struggle. Our confidence can be shattered by both seeing ourselves as outsiders in some negative sense and failing to embrace that we are unique in a very positive sense. When we see ourselves as human, we are less likely to feel like we need to be the best or like we're already the worst. We are less likely to feel victimized and more likely to look directly at our shortcomings and make real efforts to grow and change.

How To Be Confident: Get To Know Your Inner Critic

Dr. Robert Firestone, author of Overcoming the Destructive Inner Voice has written extensively about the role of the "critical inner voice" in injuring people's confidence and limiting their ability to fully be themselves. This "voice" is like a sadistic coach that attacks us from every angle and undermines our goals. It affects us in all areas of our lives. Sometimes, this destructive thought process can seem subtle, even soothing, like a parent whispering in our ear: "No need to try anything new," it says. "That will only make you anxious. Why not just stay in your comfort zone and feel safe?" Other times, that voice is outright vicious and punishing. "You literally can't do anything right. Why try? You will fail!" Whether whispering or shouting, the critical inner voice has one goal, which is to reinforce old, critical ways we have of seeing ourselves that hurt us but feel familiar, as if they're part of our identity. As Dr. Firestone put it in his blog "How to Befriend Yourself:"

The enemy within can be thought of as a negative identity. This negative identity is a byproduct of negative ways you were labeled as a child, the negative attitudes toward yourself that you incorporated from any mistreatment you were exposed to and the defensive strategies that you formed to cope with psychological pain that further bent you out of shape. You mistake the identity that you formed under these circumstances as being the truth and act as though it were. Catching on to this misconception of yourself allows you to challenge and alter this mistaken identity and can help you to become your authentic self.

Firestone has developed a series of steps people can take to help them identify and overcome their critical inner voice as well as a therapy methodology called Voice Therapy. Practicing these steps whenever our critical inner voice starts to crush our confidence is a process that can be incredibly empowering and can help bring us back to ourselves and our real, more compassionate point of view. Initially, when we challenge this inner critic (and the more we accomplish and ignore it), we may notice this voice grow even louder. However, if we're persistent and continue to cast these thoughts aside or "starve the monster," eventually, the voice will shrink down and lose power over us.

This effort to conquer our inner critic and adopt a more self-compassionate attitude is part of a lifelong process. Over and over again, we have to become aware of when that critical inner voice is creeping in and attempting to take the wheel. As we do, we can keep returning to a compassionate attitude that will help us through the hard times. In addition to this ongoing goal, there are also some actions we can take each day to boost our confidence. Here are some science-backed tips for doing just that:

* Reflect on a moments when you felt accomplished – One study recently showed that recalling an event in which we felt proud or recognized can help strengthen our confidence. These types of thoughts can also act as natural counters to our critical inner voice. These don't need to be major events – maybe just a time we were acknowledged for being generous or overcame a fear. We shouldn't get carried away, feeling like we need to pull up old victories just to believe that we're okay. Instead, we should just allow the memory itself to make us feel good and serve as a small reminder of who we really are.

 * Exercise – There's no debate that being active makes us feel good. Studies have shown that even light exercise can boost our confidence. This doesn't mean we have to do an extreme body makeover or obsess over any physical result. It just means getting moving to release some mood-boosting endorphins and enjoying the perk of feeling more confident throughout the day.

* Stand tall – Yup, that annoying reminder from teachers and parents turns out to have some merit; standing up straight can make us more confident. It may sound silly, but according to one study from Harvard and Columbia University researchers, better posture actually makes people feel more confident and powerful.

* Dress in ways that make you feel your best – No matter how minuscule our interest in fashion may be, our personal style is part of who we are. Studies have shown that how we dress can affect our performance, mood, and self-esteem, which has led some researchers to suggest that "we should put on clothes that we associate with happiness, even when feeling low."

* Practice generosity – Being generous is a natural way to reduce stress, boost one's immune system and feel a sense of purpose. Anything from volunteering to performing a favor for a friend can enhance our sense of self. "Generosity is a natural confidence builder and a natural repellent of self-hatred. Not only does it make us feel better about ourselves, but it actively combats feelings of isolation and depression," said Dr. Lisa Firestone, who co-authored Conquer Your Critical Inner Voice.

* Find tools to help reduce your anxiety – When we feel anxious, it can be very difficult to connect with feelings of confidence. There are many exercises anyone can learn to help them deal with anxiety and return a sense of inner calm and presence. We can find many techniques for alleviating anxiety here. Practicing these methods can help us feel more calm and comfortable in our skin.

Confidence is simply the degree to which you believe that your actions will result in a positive outcome.

This is not the same as self-esteem.

Self-esteem is a more general feeling you have about yourself, where as confidence is the belief you have in your skills in a given situation. When most people say they want to be more confident, what they mean is that they want more self-esteem.

Unsurprisingly however, the more areas you become confident in, the more you are likely to naturally develop self-esteem.

Why Do We Want Confidence?

Confidence is an evolutionary advantage that can help you approach whatever task is in front of you without hesitation or anxiety. It can allow us to do what we really want to do with our lives.

The problem is that most of the time the advice we get about how to be more confident can be a little generic.

"Fake it till you make it," "Talk louder" or "Dress the part."

To be fair, this isn't terrible advice, it can actually have a positive impact on how you feel, but it doesn't really instill you with the kind of deep confidence that results in real change.

Here Are 5 Hidden qualities Of Confident People.

They manage their outcome dependence

Confident people don't worry about the outcome of a situation. Their attention is focused on the action or activity as opposed to the external result.

In the event that they fail, they see it as a learning experience as opposed to a reflection of who they are as a person or even how much they're worth.

They assess themselves accurately

This might seem counter-intuitive, but to develop true confidence you need to have a little bit of brutal self-honesty.

If you have unrealistic expectations about your capabilities, you're likely to get shocked and disheartened when things don't go as you expected. On the other hand if you have an objective assessment of your skills, this is less likely to be the case.

Another important thing to consider here is that they are able to accept constructive criticism from others without getting defensive. The attention of confident people isn't focused on whether others perceive them as competent but on how they can improve for the future.

They practice Positive Visualization

Ours brains have a difficult time distinguishing real memories and constructed ones. Self-assured people use this to their advantage by visualizing their competence in a certain area until their neural networks have been rewired for success.

One study revealed that weightlifters that practiced positive visualization found the practice almost as effective as the physical practice itself for performance enhancement.

They choose their activities carefully

You can't be the best at everything and self-assured people know this. Instead they stick to what they known is going to make them confident.

For example, if they want to be a confident swimmer they might spend a lot of time running, because some of the skills are complimentary. But they're not going to spend hours writing creative stories, because the overlap between the two activities is less significant

Sometimes it's simple enough to realize that if you want to feel confident, you should spend time just doing things your confident in.

This might not be what you want to hear, but it's the truth. If you want to develop self-esteem, you need to need to push your comfort zone in a number of areas, but it is slow growth over time that will lead to deeper, long lasting confidence.

They develop their skills

To feel more confident you need to better yourself in the area you want to feel confident in, and the only way to do so is practice.

Again, this is pretty obvious, but it means being able

to focus on one area for a sustained period of time until you're competent, instead of letting your attention drift all over the place and getting what is known as 'shiny objective syndrome.'

They take action!

As Dale Carnegie said:

"Inaction breeds doubt and fear. Action breeds confidence and courage. If you want to conquer fear, do not sit home and think about it. Go out and get busy."

HOW TO USE PSYCHOLOGY
TO MOTIVATE YOURSELF

Understanding the psychology of motivation can help you when you know you need a push to get you going. When motivation is desired, there are really only two factors that will get a human being moving. The first is an anticipation of pleasure and the second is fear of pain. You can paint all kinds of pretty words around these two things like expectation of rewards or fear of reprisal, but the psychology of motivation always boils down to these same two things.

You know that when your morale is down, your productivity goes down the tubes, right. So then the best thing for you to do would be to figure out what your greatest motivators are. It is usually much healthier and less stressful to be motivated by the positive emotion of anticipation. But there are certainly those times - especially when you are under the gun - when only fear will do the trick. The key is to not let it get to that point, at least not all the time anyway.

The Psychology of Motivation Can Work For You Or Against You

Knowing that the psychology of motivation can work for you or against you, you can get yourself prepared. If you know ahead of time what it is that most motivates you, you can infuse your thinking with these ideas beforehand and keep yourself from the triple threats of procrastination, discouragement and guilt - and all the evil things that come out of them.

One of the easiest things you can do ahead of time is to take 15 or 20 minutes and write down all of the long-term goals you have. Make them juicy. Don't just write down "I want to make more money." A dollar more is still more and you know you don't just want that. If your goal is to make more money - decide what that money will get you like a cruise or an all inclusive vacation to Antigua (my personal favorite) or a fancy new car. Put a few pictures where you can easily see them and when you find yourself down think about these things and how happy they make you.

Can You "Trick" Yourself Into Feeling Motivated?

You can also use the psychology of motivation to "trick" you into feeling better and getting more done. Have you ever noticed the difference in how you feel when you are moping around compared to when you are jumping up and down excited? Big difference, right? If you want to trick yourself into feeling more motivated, just start jumping up and down and laughing. You'll get an instant boost of endorphins and it will be almost impossible to crawl back into that mopey state and you'll be more inclined to get going.

I used to believe that I simply needed to power through—use whatever energy I had left to keep working and hope for better results. But, finally, exhausted and unsatisfied with the results that I was achieving, I turned to behavioral psychology to learn how to get "unstuck" and perform at my best.

I'm going to cover the psychology behind how rewards influence our behavior and offer some techniques that you can practice to get and stay motivated.

Why We Crave Rewards

Alexander Rothman's theory of behavior maintenance suggests that your ability to maintain a positive behavior or habit is dependent on your perception of the benefits:

Decisions regarding behavioral initiation are predicted

to depend on favorable expectations regarding future outcomes, whereas decisions regarding behavioral maintenance are predicted to depend on perceived satisfaction with received outcomes.

However, challenging and ambitious projects don't always provide immediate rewards. Sometimes you even get negative feedback for prolonged periods.

When we receive positive feedback, we become more motivated. And when our motivation increases, we perform better. It's a cycle that feeds on itself.

If we perceive the rewards resulting from a given behavior as insufficient, or if we receive negative feedback, we lose motivation. This lack of motivation might manifest itself as procrastination or a lack of energy. We experience this because our brains are telling us to stop investing energy in something that is not helping us.

Douglas Lisle, a psychologist who specializes in motivation, describes moods and emotions as "feedback systems" that can indicate the effectiveness of our actions. He says that anxiety is actually an important and valuable emotion:

Anxiety is generally a useful guide—signaling us that our proposed endeavor may require our very best effort to succeed and, in fact, may require talent beyond our current abilities... The survival value of anxiety is obvious—if you are contemplating a trek across dangerous terrain, you had better be anxious. You had better consider carefully whether this is an intelligent undertaking. And, if it is, your anxiety will help to facilitate careful planning, checking and rechecking of supplies, the rehearsing of potentially needed skills, worrying about things that could go wrong, and so forth.

Anxiety is a signal that we may need to rethink our strategy. When you are overly anxious, you won't feel motivated or energized. The lack of motivation hinders your ability to perform, which hinders your ability to achieve goals.

When you're in this negative feedback loop, it's difficult to get up off the couch and get to work. You just want to sit around and do nothing. You can't seem to cross items off your to-do list, even though they've been there for weeks. But as you begin to take action and pick up small wins, you start feeling less stuck.

After making more progress, you're still not quite at your peak level of performance because there's still some uncertainty about your ability to succeed and achieve results. You still have some degree of stress, but it's healthy stress that's enough to motivate you to keep taking action. As you continue to gain momentum, you reach a state of optimal motivation and performance, before reaching a new plateau.

How We Measure Success

Behind most of the decisions we make is a cost-benefit analysis. This analysis may be done consciously or unconsciously. We compare the benefits that we expect to receive to the costs that we expect will be required.

While money is one of the most obvious forms of benefit, rewards can come in many forms. Humans also seek social status and positive feedback from peers. Rewards validate your cost-benefit analysis. It's evidence that gives you more confidence that you're moving in the right direction.

For example, say that you decide to start freelancing on the side because you're confident that you can make some extra money and build your portfolio. When you get positive feedback, in the form of a new client, your cost-benefit analysis gains validation. Your initial hypothesis, that you can start a freelancing business, is more likely to be correct.

As a result of the monetary reward from closing the new client, your cost-benefit balance further tips toward motivation (the left side of the graphic above). The benefits outweigh the costs, motivating you to continue freelancing.

Conversely, if you were to spend months trying to find a freelancing client but never manage to land one, your brain may interpret freelancing as a poor return on investment. This would limit your energy for seeking clients.

If your brain doesn't understand both the costs of inaction and the benefits of action, you won't feel very motivated.

Some people are more motivated by fear. Rather than moving toward something—such as a freelancing business—they are motivated to move away from something else. They may be motivated to get out of student debt or quit their day job. It's important to think in terms of the desired action (freelancing in this case) as well as the undesired action or the status quo. If your brain doesn't understand both the costs of inaction and the benefits of action, you won't feel very motivated.

This may seem straightforward, but it gets more interesting when you consider that we don't always do a good job of interpreting feedback. Many people don't internalize the rewards they receive. Some may even be succeeding but actually believe they're failing.

Failures can generally be grouped into two categories: real and imagined. If you have ambitious goals, you will inevitably experience a real failure. You might shut down your business, take a loss on an investment, or get dumped by a partner. However, it's far more often that your perceived failures are actually just small missteps moving you in the right direction. You simply need to reinterpret the feedback you receive.

Techniques For Boosting Motivation

Regardless of whether the negative feedback you're getting is real or imagined, there are techniques you can use to regain or sustain motivation during challenging times. Imagined failure—in the form of overreacting to negative feedback or lacking appreciation for positive feedback—can be solved through changing the way you think about your work and results. You can overcome real failure by changing your strategy.

The techniques below can help break a cycle of negative feedback and get you back into a positive feedback loop.

Change Your Thinking

Oftentimes, feelings of failure are merely figments of imagination. In these cases, you don't actually need more money or more pats on the back from your peers. Rather, you simply need to change the way you interpret your situation and internalize the rewards you're already receiving.

Set achievable goals. Studies have found that when people make progress toward goals, they are more motivated to continue. Progress reduces the perceived costs and increases confidence in future benefits. Achieving a goal also gives you data that indicates your cost-benefit analysis was correct and you are moving in the right direction. One strategy is to break big goals into smaller goals that you can achieve on a consistent basis. Your long-term goal may be to sell your company for $1 billion, but that will take years. Without some smaller wins along the way, you may lose motivation. Consider setting a weekly goal, such as shipping a new feature, or publishing a piece of content. Accomplishing shorter-term goals will keep you motivated to achieve your longer-term goals.

Acknowledge intangible rewards. According to a study by researchers at Princeton, money can make you happier, but you reach diminishing returns once you make $75,000 per year. Your biology is more concerned with simply surviving than climbing up Maslow's hierarchy of needs and realizing your full potential. Rewards such as supporting your community or increasing your financial safety net are still important. But you won't necessarily gain a dopamine hit of motivation from these things like you will from landing a new job that pays $75,000 a year. You'll need to remind yourself of the less tangible rewards you are receiving.

Change your interpretation of failure. When you fail at something, you lose motivation. Your brain tells you to stop investing time and money in an opportunity that might not lead to success. However, failure is also a learning opportunity. Now that you've failed, you know what doesn't work. You can try something new that's more likely to work. When you fail, don't identify it as a failure. Instead of telling yourself, "I'm a loser," tell yourself, "I lost this time, but I'll win in the long run." Also remember that there's an element of chance in most pursuits. The loss may not have even been a result of your performance.

Upgrade your definition of success. When you decide to start a business, your goal is probably to achieve profitability, or perhaps to sell it. However, there is a high degree of chance in starting a company. Sometimes even the most talented and hardworking entrepreneurs fail. You don't know how the economy will change, what new regulations will affect your market, how consumer preferences will shift, or what new competitors may appear. Instead of letting your motivation depend on factors outside your control, define success in terms of making good decisions and executing them to the best of your abilities.

Increase the cost of inaction. When you win at a video game, your brain thinks you've just done something beneficial, but you really haven't. Remind yourself that climbing to the top of the World of Warcraft leaderboard is not as rewarding as getting healthier, closing your next deal, or starting that nonprofit. In fact, spending too much time playing video games will only make it less likely that you will achieve your most important goals. Remind yourself that inaction has a cost and try to deprive yourself of the rewards you receive from inaction.

Change Your Behavior

Many personal development articles encourage suppressing negative emotions and forcing yourself through whatever comes your way. And, from a psychological perspective, it's easier to push through hardship than it is to accept that you are falling short. Suppressing negative feedback, though, allows you to avoid reconsidering your strategies and priorities. You may actually need less hustle and more strategic thinking.

Take on a new challenge. If the rewards you're receiving are not meeting your expectations given your perceived abilities, they may not be motivating. Lisle writes that "people sometimes become depressed because their lives no longer require their very best efforts. Consistently operating at significantly less than your full capacity may save energy, but it often doesn't feel good." Find an opportunity to take on a new project at work or start a side project that challenges you.

Change your strategy. If you're unsatisfied with the results of your efforts, consider why you are not achieving sufficient rewards and what you can do to improve. It may turn out that you are working on the right project or pursuing a great opportunity but simply need to change the way you are doing it. For example, if your blog hasn't grown the way you'd hoped, you may need to shift from writing short articles frequently to more in-depth articles less frequently. Or you may need to learn or improve a skill that can help you succeed, such as SEO or Facebook ads.

Choose the right opportunity. The cost-benefit analysis that you ran to determine what you should be working on didn't pan out as expected. This is common because it's difficult to predict the future. If you determine that you are accurately measuring your results and changing your strategy is insufficient, it may be best to shift your focus to something new. While this realization may bruise your ego, it would be foolish to deny the reality that you are not achieving the results you are capable of. Consider your strengths, weakness, and values—and find your next big opportunity.

PSYCHOLOGY AND POSITIVE THINKING

Take for example, the cell phone that has become an indispensable gadget for every one all over the world today. It too once used to be an impossible dream, however, it was the positive attitude and will of one single individual that made it possible and accessible to billions of people today. If the inventor was pessimistic and had gotten depressed with the numerous failures he might have encountered on his way, we would not be talking to our dear ones on a handy and mobile phone today. It clearly manifests the applicability of the principle that what the mind can visualize, the human body is capable of achieving it.

Ones Psychology and Positive Thinking play a crucial role in countering negative tendencies

The feeling of joy born out of a positive and healthy existence is unbeatable. Ones life condition becomes such that one feels lively, happy and capable of taking on anything in this world. The future looks all bright and brimming with hope and fulfillment. One feels the thankfulness of being alive from ones core. Life just looks perfect - flawless!

In reality, however, it all sounds to good to be true.

The people nowadays are surrounded by so many worries and fears stemming from various issues related to relationships, finance, career, family life, office etc. that taking out time to think positively becomes a rare activity. Positive thinking by its very meaning is all about the state of one?s mind rather than one?s actions. Of course the state of mind eventually gets manifested in the form of actions, but it all starts from ones brain. You must firmly believe and be confident about the fact that you are endowed with all sorts of capabilities, health and attitude to taste success. This is also known as positive affirmation.

A synonym often used for positive affirmation is self-suggestion. However, self-suggestion refers to the method by which one can rid oneself of all the negative thoughts that stop him/her from thinking positive. Subjecting oneself to repeated self-suggestions can work wonders on the individual by leading him/her to a life state full of positive thoughts.

You can even opt for the strategy of recording all your self-suggestions and positive affirmations on a CD with a background music score and playing it regularly while driving to work or when relaxing. This method helps immensely in driving certain thoughts home and ensuring their absorption and manifestation in a very successful manner.

Positive Thinking - A Self-Learning Process

It is often commented in the psychology parlance that what the mind visualizes, body is capable to achieve. It is the mind that is the center of ones existence and determines all the actions of a person. Thus, if you are able to visualize success in you mind, your body and your surroundings start working towards the accomplishment of that goal in a very spontaneous manner. The more positive thoughts you feed your mind with, the more positive results you will see in your environment.

It is very important that you do not confuse positive thinking with daydreaming. Positive thinking is much more rooted in the reality of our day-to-day existence as compared to dreaming. It instills in us the ability to respond to the situations in a positive manner, thus helping us change the circumstances for better.

Another great benefit that you stand to gain from the habit of positive thinking is that it will help you through the difficult times of your life. So even when the tides are not in your favor, you will be able to derive the strength to keep pushing on and emerge victorious over yourself.

Understanding the Psychology of Positive Thinking

You may have heard about positive thinking, but don't really know enough about to know exactly how it works. Positive thinking can provide many benefits in your life such as improving your health, opportunities in life, the way you relate to others and the way you see yourself.

The psychology behind the power of positive thinking is that you're more apt to take on life with a positive outlook and have more positive results than if you face the world negatively. That doesn't mean that you should gloss over the obvious, but it does mean that a bad circumstance can be made much brighter than viewing them in a negative way.

Some psychologists view positive thinking as how you explain what happens in your life. If you have an optimistic attitude, you're more likely to explain away bad things that happen by blaming something else for the circumstance. You're also more apt to view a negative happening as outside the norm or a temporary circumstance.

Abraham Lincoln once commented, "Most folks are about as happy as they make up their minds to be."

Abraham Lincoln once commented, "Most folks are

about as happy as they make up their minds to be."

When you make up your mind to approach life's challenges with a positive attitude, you're not ignoring the bad stuff in the world, but it does mean that you're attempting to see the best both in people and in situations.

Positive thinking and positive psychology are often thought to be the same, but they're really not. With positive psychology, the focus is definitely on positive thinking, but most psychologists tend to think it's more beneficial to think realistically.

For example, positive thinking might lead a person to take risks that he or she shouldn't, such as investing money in a business that's extremely risky or thinking positively that you can swim across the lake without taking into consideration the distance.

However, it is clear that thinking more positively will ensure more positive outcomes in your life. The best thing you can do is to pay attention to your self-talk and realistically assess whether it's better to think that way – or not.

Health Benefits

In recent years, the so-called "power of positive thinking" has gained a great deal of attention thanks to self-help books such as The Secret. While these pop-psychology books often tout positive thinking as a sort of psychological panacea, empirical research has found that there are many very real health benefits linked to positive thinking and optimistic attitudes.

According to the Mayo Clinic, positive thinking is linked to a wide range of health benefits including:

- ✓ Longer life span

- ✓ Less stress

- ✓ Lower rates of depression

- ✓ Increased resistance to the common cold

- ✓ Better stress management and coping skills

- ✓ Lower risk of cardiovascular disease-related death

- ✓ Increased physical well-being

- ✓ Better psychological health

One study of 1,558 older adults found that positive thinking could also reduce frailty during old age.

Clearly, there are many benefits of positive thinking, but why exactly does positive thinking have such a strong impact on physical and mental health.

One theory is that people who think positively tend to be less affected by stress. Another possibility is that people who think positively tend to live healthier lives in general; they may exercise more, follow a more nutritious diet and avoid unhealthy behaviors.

As you practice positive thinking, you'll become more adept at culling out the positive thoughts that aren't realistic as opposed to the thoughts that can have a positive impact on your life.

POSITVE THIKING VS POSITIVE PSYCHOLOGY

Affirmations in the New Age movement refer to the belief that the practice of positive thinking and holding a positive attitude are strong enough to allow anyone to achieve success in anything they do. The Secret has been the moving force in this believe system, as it has been advocated and supported by millions.

Everyone from Oprah, to Big Sean, to Montel has claimed The Secret works and has encouraged everyone to do the same. Positive Psychology is not the same as positive thinking and or affirmations and it is one of the largest misconceptions of this field, especially with the rise of the New Age movement.

In fact, some positive psychology researchers, such as Barbara Fredrickson, argue that it is detrimental to have insincere positive emotions and thoughts, as it will eventually backfire.

In the last decade, we have also seen the growth of positive psychology, a new branch of mental science which looks at the sunnier side of life (the study of human flourishing.) Positive psychology focuses on positive aspects of wellbeing including (but not limited to) positive emotions, happiness, hope, optimism and other constructs that relate to the idea of positive thinking.

To the uninformed, it would be easy to assume that positive psychology and positive thinking are strongly related. Some might even say, "Finally, science is proving what we have always thought to be true about positive thinking." But this is not exactly the case. While positive thinking and positive psychology may be related, they are more like third cousins than twin brothers. And anyone who uses one or the other would be benefited by understanding the differences:

Philosophical orientation: Positive thinking begins with the assumption that positive thinking is good for you. This is often based on personal or anecdotal experience and then extrapolated to other aspects of life as a general prescription for a better life. Positive psychology begins with scientific inquiry. Positive psychology takes some of those assumptions about positive thinking and says, "let's test them" to see where they hold true or don't.Ich liebe dich...

Positive thinking proponents, for example, argue that positivity is a powerful factor in our health and recovery from illness. Positive psychology has also found a strong link between happiness and health but seeks to understand the limitations of this relationship. Positive emotions seem to help more with prevention than with cure, and more with lifestyle illnesses than with genetic or environmental ones.

Positive emotions help build our social support network, encourage more positive lifestyle choices and buffer us from the negative health impacts of stress. But there are many serious health issues that positive emotions have little impact on. In fact, too much optimism could discourage people from seeking the treatment they need. Positive psychology is about using the scientific method to understand these nuances.

Positivity ratios: Positive thinking generally promotes the "more is better" approach to positivity. Some proponents of positive thinking would argue that if you don't have the wealth, health or happiness you want out of life, it's because you allowed some negativity to creep in. Only by shutting these thoughts out and focusing on the positive can you be successful.

Positive psychology on the other hand, is about understanding the purpose of positive emotions and understanding the different contexts when they may prove valuable. Positive psychology is also interested in negative emotions when they help us to flourish in our lives. Barbara Fredrickson, for example, a researcher who specializes in positive emotions, has found an ideal ratio of 3 positive emotions to every 1 negative emotion for human flourishing. 3:1, not 3:0.

Many researchers in positive psychology are studying the benefits of mindfulness, which means accepting both positive and negative emotions (in whatever ratio they happen to exist) and then acting consciously, while staying true to personal values and goals. These researchers argue for the importance of a meaningful life over a happy one.

Optimism

positive thinking eschews an optimistic outlook even when one isn't warranted by the situation. Proponents will suggest "affirmations" for example, where people are told to say out loud things they wish to be true, even if they aren't (e.g. "I make a million dollars a year!") Positive psychology studies why optimism is sometimes beneficial (and sometimes not.) Psychology researchers don't generally promote uninhibited optimism in all situations.

As Martin Seligman, the author of Learned Optimism, says, "you don't want the pilot who is de-icing the wings of your plane to be an optimist." Another psychologist, Sandra Schneider, promotes "realistic optimism," which is a matter of trying to realistically get to the truth of a matter, but where ambiguity lies in the meaning of a situation, favor the more positive assumption that will bring you greater mental wellbeing.

Another researcher Acacia Parks, says that the positive psychology brand of optimism is not about being positive all the time but about "entertaining the possibility that things could work out." The benefit of optimism comes from being open to it, not from blindly following it even when it makes no sense to do so.

The reality is, much of what the positive thinking movement has proposed has shown some validity, and this is why people do get benefit out of reading The Secret or attending Tony Robbins' seminars. Barbara Fredrickson has identified "upward spirals" to show how our positive emotions tend to reverberate off of those around us, sustaining and amplifying their benefits. And Martin Seligman has studied the benefits of favoring more optimistic thinking styles. But positive thinking is a one-note song that falls flat in certain situations, while positive psychology is about understanding the rich complexity of the positive side of life.

THE POWER OF POSITIVE THINKING

Many times today people undermine the power of positive thinking. Most people never truly understand the power that positive thoughts have over our every day lives. It's these same people who believe that success comes from something outside of themselves and most seem to have a hard time creating success in their lives. I have created this article to talk you about the concept and power of positive thinking and how I have implemented certain basic pre-school techniques that have truly enhanced my life in every way, shape, and form.

I started my journey on to positive thinking and personal development through reading everyday. Reading is a powerful medium all in it's own. I read biographies and auto-biographies of some of the most successful people in the world. I started reading these types of books because I wanted to see how these people created success in their lives. As I began reading these books I noticed something amazing. Each successful person, no matter their field of study, utilized a certain step by step process that empowered them to first think positively then bring those positive thoughts into reality.

It may not be a new piece of advice to have someone

telling you that you will succeed in life as long as you think positive. However, is the power of positive thinking so strong that you will be guaranteed of success if you do not harbour negative thoughts in your mind? You may be surprise but the answer is a resounding 'Yes!' and today you will learn how having a positive mindset can bring you greater success in life.

As Buddha once said, "What You Have Become Is What You Have Thought", so you need to be positive in your thinking in order to attract the positive energies from the universe. Having a positive mindset means that you will not give up easily and that is especially important if you run a business. It will also affect your relationship with the people around you. It might not be an easy task to change your thoughts to being positive if you are someone who is not optimistic. However, if you want to achieve your dreams, you have to work on it because your mindset will directly affect your life.

The power of positive thinking has been around for many decades and there have been numerous studies done to prove that there is a direct relationship between what you think and the results you get at the end. I am sure you have heard of terminally ill cancer patients who recover miraculously because of their positive mindset and strong belief that they will survive.

Positive thinking has a new advocate these days. Dr. David R. Hawkins is a leading psychiatrist who has published numerous books about the power of positive thinking as well as the power of many forms of thought and spiritual teachings. Using the findings of kinesiology, Dr. Hawkins has made it easier to determine the power of positive thinking versus negative thinking and has shown how many people can alter their lives for the better. By using certain muscle testing techniques, Dr. Hawkins kinesiological research has helped to determine that certain systems of thought are actually more powerful than others in promoting the health and well being of all people.

According to the studies done with kinesiology, various statements, teachings, teachers and subjects of interest all carry a certain energy field along with their subject matter. When these different topics are held in mind by individuals, the reactions of their muscles are then monitored and can determine various strengths and levels of power in the fields present. Through the observation of the muscles reactions, scientists can determine if the individual statements evoke a positive reaction in the muscles or not. This has been shown to be useful in determining the actual power of some statements as opposed to others and of various persons, places or things as they affect the energy meridians in the body. The research is extremely beneficial to those who have examined the findings and has even spurned more studies which are all continuing today.

Dr. Hawkins has gone even further with his research than the simple testing of statements and their relative power. He has devised a scale of consciousness which can actually be used to determine the level of power for anything anywhere and he has used the reaction of the muscles to determine those levels of power according to the science of kinesiology. First, a scale of power was set up from 0 to 1000 and tested subjects were told that zero represented the absolutely lowest level or "no power" range. The highest level at 1000 represented the most power possible level for a human being to be capable of acquiring and the scale was set up as logarithmic so that it was representative of an increase in terms of exponential increments. Many statements, patterns of thought and even teachings were all proven again and again to have a certain level of power according to their kinesiological response in the body.

In terms of the power of positive thinking, there have been many teachers and teachings which have been reported to score very high on the consciousness scale. Among some of the higher numbers were teachers such as the Buddha, Jesus and Krishna who all scored very high with all test subjects. Similarly, many Eastern teachers such as Ramana Maharshi, Nisargadatta Maharaj and Muktananda all scored in the 600 is and 700 is in terms of the way peoples bodies reacted to the teachings. The word "Love" has consistently scored extremely high at 500 and the word "peace" was also scored at 600. These findings were astounding and have become part of a widespread study and a series of publications which are now very popular in many countries. It is clear from these findings that there is an inherent power to positive thinking which can actually have a physical affect on your body if it is repeated and made to become part of your lifestyle. The findings of Dr. Hawkins suggest a number of things, one of which is that nothing is thought to have come about as a result of an accident or a "random" occurrence. Each thing carries with it a field of energy which largely affects the outcome of its existence. With the discovery that everything carries with it a certain level of power, it is also the case that nothing can be said to be part of an accident unless we were to ignore the recently discovered designations that have been made upon these various objects or thought patterns. Individual people themselves can be tested to be holding a certain amount of energy or "power" such that the reactions of the muscles can also show this level of power in many circumstances. With this discovery, brings the obvious conclusion that, not only are certain thoughts more or less powerful but everything which is capable of being held in mind is subject to a certain test of power.

We all must be aware of the law of attraction, which can show us how to feel positively about a certain topic or subject and it is these thoughts within us that influence how we feels, which is what makes us get attracted to something that we desire. For most people, being able to say that the product that they are selling is great is very easy, but when the same people are alone, it is not that easy to feel and think positively because they may be more preoccupied with worrying about paying their bills or having to play a role in which they will need to decide how to react under negative circumstances.

So, to harness the power of positive thinking and be full of optimism and have a bright outlook requires paying close attention to your innermost thoughts and being able to focus on being aware of these thoughts and learning to direct them in a direction where they are most needed, which is really a manifestation of feeling positive rather than negative. Having a positive attitude and being attentive to positive thoughts isn't something that is taught to us as children and it is not a natural expression of our inner self. In fact, it is common to be careful about what we are saying and not pay enough attention to what are our thoughts.

The Law of Attraction works with the power of thoughts and feelings. What you think of most is what happens most. Now just imagine if you could create pathways of only positive thoughts in your brain. That will attract only more positive things in your life. Start focusing on positive thoughts to experience the power of positive thinking.

'Nothing is good or bad but thinking makes it so'. Our ancestors had discovered this secret. Now you have the chance to use it to its fullest potential. Stay in the moment. Stop accepting everything you hear around you.

The Healing Power Of Positive Thinking With Mind Power

Do you remember when you were sick last? I'm sure it felt horrible. And, what's worse, as you develop illness, big or small, you eventually succumb to negative thoughts as you unconsciously stare the sickness down into the illnesses beady little eyes. You focus on the illness. It usually happens as you permit our thoughts to focus on what's wrong, the negative. Now, try to remember when a loved one looks after you and continues to assure you that you will get better soon. You shift your focus on the healthy, more positive future and you lose site of the negative aspect, you only have positive thoughts.

Positive thinking is no medical miracle, no quick fix pill that eliminates all illnesses instantly. But, in a short time, comparatively, you're better. The same concept is used in placebo medicine, it's as if it causes your mind to have a strong belief that everything is going to be alright and you are going to get better soon. This is the power of Positive thoughts, the belief that you will get better, and along with the real results or the implied results from the medicine, this work hand in hand for a positive result.

There's been test after tests, researches after researches about the power of positive thinking on healing. Most studies have proven that positive thoughts can indeed speed up a persons healing.

There was a scientific research done to see how a

persons thoughts can impact their health. It was proven that when people are stressed, our ability to fight off illnesses or diseases, the immune system of the body, gets weaker. Now, when that same person transforms their thoughts to a positively nature, hence minimizing their stress, the immune system strengthens.

Here are few tips to attain positive thinking:

1) Feel Positive - let positive feelings flow through you. Use mental images (go to your happy place). Find the feeling of happiness, success and strength.

2) Be Near Positive - surround yourself with people who positive and just in their thoughts but in their actions also. It can be contagious, either Positive or negative feelings. Being around those whose moods are negative, the glass is half empty people can also make your spirits negative. But bring those positive folks around whose outlook on life is positive then so will yours. Remember, you are the sum total of the people you surround yourself with!

3) Say Positive, Think Positive - Hear Positive, Think Positive. Always use positive words and listen to positive music, not only when speaking but also when you are thinking. Words like "I am capable" and "I can" are powerful mood changers.

Growing a positive thought process is the key to inner self-healing. It's not that easy to do, especially when we are always around negative people but it is do-able. A positive outlook in life will empower you, motivate you, even if your situation or circumstances is far from where or what you want it to be, just be positive and you can expect positive results, even if it is only in your spirit. Guaranteed, with a positive adjustment to your life, your life will change.

In self-healing by thinking positive, I should also say that you should still need to seek out the help of a doctor for that professional opinion and advice, when you are not feeling well. I'm also not advising to not take medicines anymore and that all you need is to think positive about your condition and you'll get better. I'm trying to tell you to use positive thinking side by side with your current treatment.

If you are being treated and you are also in a negative thought process about your life and condition, you will definitely get worse. On the other hand, if you are in an unfortunate state of affair and you focus on positive thinking side by side with your treatment, then it will seriously strengthen your odds dramatically. Your thoughts and your mind and have enormous power on your body and life!

7 Ways To Increase Positive Thinking

A positive thinking pattern is a thought process that helps you approach everything in life in a more productive, positive way, thinking only the best will happen to you. Here are 7 ways to increase your sense of optimism and boost your positive outlook on life:

1. Positive Self talk:

One of the best positive thinking tips, positive self talk can help you change the way you think and talk to your mind.

Filling your mind with positive thoughts and conveying positive messages to your brain can help you gradually kick negativity out of your life. Immediately say "Stop" when you notice yourself thinking of negativity and pessimism.

Saying this aloud will be even more helpful, which will make you aware as to how many times you are shunning negative thoughts that may run through your head innumerable times every day.

2. Change limiting beliefs:

When you say you can't or won't do something, you are only building up resistance against doing that thing.

Remember, self-limiting beliefs cannot do you any good. Challenge yourself every time you entertain such a belittling thought or belief, changing "I can't" to "why can't I." Start saying I can and you will notice a huge difference in your thought processes, clearing the way for positive thoughts to set in!

3. Replace negative influences:

One of the simplest ways to change positive thinking is to replace negative influences with positive ones.

If you are constantly surrounded by people who are always negative, you tend to adopt their thoughts gradually and become a victim of negativity without conscious choice on your part.

Limit your exposure to such people, who do not speak encouraging words and are always unsupportive of your goals and dreams. Surround yourself with positive and successful minds, who always inspire and motivate you to face and deal with challenges and obstacles in life.

Such people vibrate positive energy that will inspire you to entertain positive thoughts and think positive for yourself too.

4. Focus on the present:

Ask yourself, "Can I change my past"?

The answer will be No, because you cannot control or change what has already happened.

However, you can always control your future. You can learn from your past and tell yourself that you can influence your future and won't repeat your mistakes again. Thus such positive thinking will certainly help you build a better tomorrow.

Be grateful for everything you have at present. A state of contentment and gratitude can sometimes do wonders to your psyche, and can change how to tackle the issues in your life with better clarity.

5. Focus on happy moments:

When you remember happy moments, it eases stress. Remember, there are happy and sad moments in everybody's life.

Tell yourself that everybody must face ups and downs in life. Make it a conscious habit to remember good events, rather than difficult times.

6. Read books or watch movies:

When you think negative thoughts, you tend to believe that the worst happens with you alone.

But if you read inspiring books and quotes or watch inspirational movies, you realize that the greatest men on earth even had to overcome troubles and hardships before they have attained great success and wealth.

Reading motivational books or biographies of successful people will help flood your mind with good thoughts and encourage you to develop positive thinking skills as well.

7. Learn to Meditate:

Meditation is one of the best ways to increase positive thinking and clarity. It allows you to connect with your inner self and change your thought pattern, clearing your soul of negativity.

A great quote by Buddha said, "The mind is everything. What you think you become." If you can transform your thought process, you can control everything that transpires in your life.

PSYCHOLOGY AND MINDFULNESS

There is growing interest in the applications of mindfulness in applied psychological settings. However, the speed at which it is being assimilated by Western psychological and public healthcare disciplines has led to concerns about whether the evidence for mindfulness-based interventions justifies this growing popularity. Concerns have also been raised over the 'authenticity' of contemporary Western approaches and whether they bear any resemblance to the traditional Buddhist model. This article examines these issues and discusses whether the current popularity of mindfulness is likely to be just a passing trend, or 'a breath of fresh air' in terms of alleviating suffering and advancing understanding of the human mind.

Research into the attributes, correlates, and applications of mindfulness has increased greatly during recent decades. In fact, mindfulness is arguably one of the fastest-growing areas of psychological research. During 2013 almost 600 scientific papers concerning mindfulness were published, representing a tenfold increase compared to the number of mindfulness papers published during 2003 (Shonin et al., 2013a).

However, due to the speed at which mindfulness has been taken out of its traditional Buddhist setting and assimilated by Western psychological and medical disciplines, concerns and integration issues have inevitably arisen. One such concern is whether the quality of empirical evidence tallies with the numerous claims concerning the efficacy and utility of mindfulness-based interventions (MBIs).

This article briefly discusses current empirical research directions and provides what we believe is timely critical opinion on key issues in mindfulness research, including whether the current popularity of mindfulness in psychology is likely to be just a passing trend, or 'a breath of fresh air' in terms of advancing understanding of the human mind.

Our life can quickly pass us by when we're not focused on what matters. We have a bad habit of emphasizing the negative and overlooking the positive. Being mindful can help. Mindfulness is a state of active, open attention on the present. When we are mindful, we carefully observe our thoughts and feelings without judging them as good or bad. Mindfulness can also be a healthy way to identify and manage hidden emotions that may be causing problems in our personal and professional relationships. It means living in the moment and awakening to our current experience, rather than dwelling on the past or anticipating the future. Mindfulness is frequently used in meditation and certain kinds of therapy. It has many positive benefits, including lowering stress levels, reducing harmful ruminating, improving our overall health, and protecting against depression and anxiety. There is even research suggesting that mindfulness can help people cope better with rejection and social isolation.

A person's experience of time tends to be subjective and is heavily influenced by their emotional state. Fears and insecurities about the past and the future can make it difficult to fully enjoy the present. The key is learning how to pay attention and focus on the here and now. Mindfulness is a tool that allows people to be more aware of their physical and emotional conditions without getting bogged down in self-criticism and judgment. Mindfulness done well allows one to regain control over destructive feelings and even to capture positive memories that can be savored at a later date.

What Is Mindfulness and How Does It Work?

You may have heard the term "Mindfulness" and have a rough idea of what it's about but in this article, you'll get a very clear understanding of what it is and why it's important to you.

With the growth of mindfulness meditation as an intervention for stress, tension, anxiety, depression, pain, rumination, sleeplessness, and many other common ailments, this is quickly becoming a big question arising all over North America and world wide.

Mindfulness is that gap where you, the awareness, are aware of what's happening within your mind. You become clear and alert to what you think, say and do. Often people meditate as a way of being clearer without all the distractions the flood through the senses. However, becoming aware of your breath and focusing on the air flowing in and out of the lungs can also do it.

This may not sound like any big deal, but it's a monumental leap of what any other creature can do. Humans are the only species on this planet that can do this. This is because every other species doesn't identify with the mind to create an ego, they simply accept things as they are and are one with it.

For example, a cat doesn't sit there and think, what does that human think of me, should I make my coat shinier so that he'll pat me and give me food? No, they simply accept this moment and do what they do through instinct and being in alignment with the present moment.

In this way animals have an advantage over humans, but what we have is the next phase of evolution, where we have an amazing capacity to not only survive but also thrive like no other species.

The issue is though, our quest to survive and thrive has become out of balance with our essential nature of oneness with all. This imbalance causes us to experience pain, which ultimately leads us to not only search for but also to find what the Truth is for us. It's life's way of restoring balance and when you consider that we are not separate to life, it's our way of restoring balance within ourselves.

So can you see why this is important now?

In a nutshell, the illusion of living day to day through entirely mind based activity (usually in hope or in fear that tomorrow will be different than today) causes pain, NOW. The way to begin to find your way through the pain is to bring awareness to your breath and from there, seeing what you think, say and do. The awareness creates a gap between you and what is perceived and through that a choice can be made for what is real, you the awareness or what your mind is telling you through a perception!

When you go on a binge, just before you start you always have these overwhelming feelings of cravings for food. Before starving yourself you have feelings of aversion or disgust with yourself and your body - so you stop eating.

With mindfulness you will be able to see your eating disorder as a foreign voice (or a person) who is sitting inside you, telling you what to do. When you practice mindfulness you will be able to separate yourself from this foreign voice and be free.

Mindfulness is a subset of meditation practices. To be mindful first of all you must learn to meditate. Mindfulness and meditation are similar but not exactly the same. Like we have already explained that mindfulness is the awareness of the present moment. But Meditation is the intentional self regulation of attention. During meditation you regulate and control your attention. And this is a development of mindfulness.

In mindfulness you learn not to judge and not to react. Observing what passes by nonjudgmentally, from moment to moment, with no reactivity whatsoever towards any part of the experience, whether the thought or the sensation. By decreasing our overactivity in the judgmental part of the mind and the reactive part of the mind, our nervous system learns to change its pattern. It becomes less judgmental, less reactive, more objective, providing us with more opportunities to manage life whatever the problem is.

This method is not limited to eating disorders, anxieties, fears or depression. People of different faiths practice this method in different ways for thousands of years. This is certainly not limited to psychological or emotional problems.

Everyone will benefit from decreasing reactivity, decreasing biased judgments, giving new parameters to the nervous system, and more insight and focused attention. In a nutshell, the purpose of practicing mindfulness training is to develop a degree of acceptance towards one's experience, and of course an equal degree of awareness. When things become acceptable on the inside, it seems that people find things more acceptable on the outside as well. The world becomes a better place.

How Mingling Mindfulness With Positive Psychology Makes You Great

According to a recent study, the key to our survival as a species is the survival of the kindest, not merely the fittest. Thus, having kindness as the dominant trait in a person would be key to both evolution and personal successes. Another recent study reveals that mixing both mindfulness and positive psychology would result in optimized well-being and elevate one's compassionate trait and resistance to stress and negativity.

With resistance to stress and negativity, we can be our best selves, hence being a "super human," who can achieve many things and be useful to society. With minimal stress and negativity in aggregate, assuming billions of individuals are also in this state of mind, civilization can progress positively.

Now, let's discuss the theory of "survival of the kindest," what mindfulness and positive psychology are, their benefits, how they're linked with each other, and how to integrate them in life to eliminate stress and negativity.

Survival of the Kindest

According to Dacher Keltner, the director of the Berkeley Social Interaction Laboratory, in his book, Born to Be Good: The Science of a Meaningful Life, the evolution has crafted the human species that comes with remarkable tendencies toward generosity, kindness, reverence, self-sacrifice, and play. They play important roles in survival, gene replication, and smooth functioning.

Despite the misconception that violence, competitiveness, and self-interest were the natural state of human beings, which were responsible for our evolution, Charles Darwin, on the contrary, had a different understanding. Darwin argued that human beings' tendencies toward compassionate social instincts were stronger than the instinct of self-preservation. Otherwise, our species would have been extinct already, which says a lot about the survival of the kindest.

The Link between Mindfulness and Positive Psychology

According to Vago and Silbersweig in Frontiers in Human Neuroscience:

mindfulness is a trait or mental state involving intentional focusing of the attention on an object, like breathing, while observing thoughts, emotions, and sensations as they emerge in the present moment.

Mindfulness itself is beneficial to health in five ways: attention regulation, increased body awareness, emotional regulation, emotional-exposure regulation, and changes in the perspective of the self.

Positive Psychology is the scientific study of the positive traits that enable individuals and communities to thrive. It was pioneered by Martin Seligman in 1998 and was also co-initiated by Mihaly Czikszentmihalyi and Christopher Peterson. This new field of psychology isn't based on pathology model. Instead, it's based on the belief that people want to lead meaningful and fulfilling lives by cultivating their best selves.

The practice of mindfulness is used as one of the tools of positive psychology, as it has been linked to increased positive feelings, a greater sense of coherence, improved quality of life, greater empathy, greater satisfaction in relationships, and more hope (Vago and Silbersweig, 2012). Other tools include gratitude journaling, reframing from negativity to positivity, self-compassion, and listing personal strengths.

Another link between mindfulness and positive psychology is that mindfulness increases well-being and positive mental qualities, including compassion. Mindfulness-based meditation has been used in compassion training, which would result in increased sensitivity to one's self and others' needs. By being empathetic, we would be more motivated to help others. In return, this facilitates greater compassion and gives us feelings of joy and satisfaction. In other words, they create a circle of joy (Cebolla, 2017).

Integrating Mindfulness and Positive Psychology in Life

Once we've been able to create and close the positive circle and repeated the process in loops, negativity and stress would diminish over time. It's probably something like the antithesis of depression. Thus, it allows for optimized activities, both in quality and quantity.

It might sound like a utopia that combining mindfulness and positive psychology would make us "super humans." However, many educators are already teaching mindfulness in elementary classrooms worldwide.

Studies have shown that mindfulness taught since childhood would do more than increased positivity, greater compassion, and diminishing stress and negativity. It would also help with focus, emotion regulation, engagement, and future career satisfaction, which would solve many problems.

You can begin with integrating mindfulness meditation, walking meditation, gratitude journaling, reminding ourselves of our strengths and positive traits, self-compassion, and reframing negativity with positivity. It doesn't require any money to begin, just a motivation to start and turn the activities into a lifelong habit.

As Einstein once said:

We cannot solve our problems with the same thinking we used when we created them.

We've found the answer. With greater positivity and compassion, the world's problems can be solved. And it starts with one person: You.

7 Great Benefits of Mindfulness in Positive Psychology

In the most basic sense, mindfulness is being consciously aware of your thoughts and emotions. For one to practice good mindfulness it involves the 'self-regulation' of attention so that it is focused on adopting a neutral attitude toward one's experiences in the present moment.

There are many beneficial effects on developing and practicing mindfulness. Below are 7 great benefits of mindfulness.

1. Being mindful of your thoughts and emotions promotes well-being

The concept of self-regulation is somewhat paradoxical in that regulation in the strictest sense of the word such as self-control is not 'mindful'. Rather, mindfulness is a state that is characterized by introspection, openness, reflection and acceptance of oneself.

Recently in the field of psychology, there has been strong evidence demonstrating that mindfulness is significantly correlated with positive affect, life satisfaction, and overall well-being.

Mindfulness itself, however, is not a new concept; it has existed in Buddhism for over two thousand of years. Modern day research has made several interesting findings suggesting this 'enhanced self-awareness' diminishes stress and anxiety and, in turn, reduces the risk of developing cancer, disease, and psychopathology. It is useful to practice mindfulness in positive psychology as a tool for general physical and mental health.

2. Being mindful can improve your working memory

Working memory is the memory system that temporarily stores information in our minds for further recall and future processing. Many studies have been undertaken that suggest a strong interrelationship between attention and working memory.

van Vugt & Jha (2011) undertook research that involved taking a group of participants to an intensive month-long mindfulness retreat. These participants were compared with a control group who received no mindfulness training (MT). All participants from both groups first undertook a memory recognition task before any MT had been providing. The second round of a memory recognition task was then undertaken by all participants after the month's training.

Results were positive – while accuracy levels were comparable across both groups, reaction times were much faster for the group that had received mindfulness training. These results suggested that MT leads to attentional improvements, particularly in relation to quality of information and decisional processes, which are directly linked to working memory.

mindfulness vs depressive symptoms3. Mindfulness acts as a buffer against the depressive symptoms associated with discrimination

A self-report study conducted at the University of North Carolina measured the level of discrimination experienced by participants and also the presence and/or severity of their depressive symptoms. Participants also completed a questionnaire that measured their level of mindfulness as a trait, which is characterized by a conscious awareness of the present.

The results showed that the more discrimination participants experienced the more depressive symptoms they had. It was also found that the more mindful people were, the less depressed they were.

Finally, and most importantly, the findings suggested that mindfulness might be a protective factor that mitigates the effects of discrimination on the development of depressive symptoms. That is, although discrimination was associated with depressive symptoms, the association became much weaker as mindfulness increased. So, it appears that practicing mindfulness may be one way of preventing the onset of depression!

4. Mindfulness can help you make better use of your strengths

"Mindfulness can help an individual express their character strengths in a balanced way that is sensitive to the context and circumstance they are in."(Niemiec, 2012)

A lot of research has shown that mindfulness influences mental health and personality (Baer, Smith

& Allen, 2004). Not surprisingly, mindfulness is related to character strengths as well.

Mindfulness and Strengths

Mindfulness and strengths joined forces a long time ago. In Buddhism, mindfulness meditation not only relieves suffering but also cultivates positive characteristics and strengths such as compassion, wisdom, and well-being. Even the meaning of mindfulness, defined by Thich Nhat Hanh (Niemiec, 2014), includes some dimensions of strengths. He saw mindfulness as a means "to keep one's attention alive in the present reality. And this 'aliveness' captures both the self-regulation of attention and the approach of curiosity."

Relationship of Mindfulness and Strengths

According to research by Bishop and colleagues (2004), experiencing mindfulness begins with making a commitment to maintain curiosity about the mind wandering and looking at differences in other objects.

Other research (Ivtzan, Gardner & Smailova, 2011) found that curiosity is one of the strengths that is correlated to living a satisfied, meaningful, and engaging life.

According to a study by Niemiec, Rashid & Spinella (2012), transcendence strengths can become more meaningful in mindfulness practice as they connect mindfulness with spiritual meaning.

In addition, during the practice of mindfulness, people may face both internal and external obstacles including boredom, wandering mind, physical discomfort, and difficulty in commitment, and this requires the strength of courage and perseverance to overcome and keep going.

Mindfulness, strengths, and acknowledgment

"Mindfulness opens a door of awareness to who we are and character strengths are what is behind the door since character strengths are who we are at core" (Niemiec, 2014)

Mindfulness can help you make better use of your strengths. One needs attention to their inner states and behavior to pursue a goal (Brown, Ryan & Creswell, 2007). Therefore, to be able to see your strength, you need to access your inner state of mind. To access your strengths or your true self, mindfulness is the path.

Research by Carlson (20013) showed that we have many blind spots, such as information barrier and motivation barrier, which is modest and meager in self-evaluation. It also decreases the bias we have in ourselves since practicing mindfulness reduces the defensiveness of your ego as you start to have more reality-based thoughts.

Mindfulness and Neuroplasticity

The term neuroplasticity refers to structural and functional changes in the brain related to experience. It has been known that musical training and language learning promote structural changes in our brain and cognitive abilities.

Mindful awareness is a form of experience that changes not only structure, but also the function of our brain throughout our lives.

You can think of mindfulness as a mental muscle. Every time we lift weight, we strengthen the muscle we are working on. In the same way, every time we pay attention to the present moment without judgment, connectivity of the attention, self-regulation and compassion circuitry grows in our brain.

5. Mindfulness practice raises your happiness set-point

Our brain is divided into left and right hemispheres. It has been shown that our brain has high activity in the right prefrontal cortex (front part of the brain) when we are in a depressed, anxious mood.

Our brain has high activity in left prefrontal cortex when we are happy and energetic. This ratio of left-to-right activity shows our happiness set-point throughout daily activities. So, what happens to this ratio when we practice mindfulness meditation?

The research of Richard Davidson and Jon Kabat-Zinn shows that only 8-week of 1-hour daily mindfulness practice leads to significant increase in left-sided activation in the brain and this increase is maintained even after 4 months of the training program (Davidson, Kabat-zinn et al., 2003). In brief, this finding demonstrates that short-term mindfulness practice increases our happiness level significantly, even at a physical level.

"Short-term mindfulness practice increases our happiness level significantly"

6. It makes you more resilient

Resilience, in most basic terms, is individual's ability to recover from setbacks and adapt well to change. Similarly, in our brain, we have a region called anterior cingulate cortex (ACC), located deep inside our forehead. ACC plays important role in self-regulation and learning from the past experience to promote optimal decision making.

The research findings of Tang and his colleagues show that mindfulness training groups that went through only 3-hour practice have higher activity in ACC and also show higher performance on the tests of self-regulation and resisting distractors, compared to the control group (Tang et al., 2007, 2009). This means that with the help of mindfulness practice, we can change our brain in the way we react to setbacks and make decisions in our life.

7. It shrinks the stress region in your brain

Remember that time you rush through life with sweat palms and trouble sleeping at night? Every time we get stressed, the 'amygdala' takes over control.

Amygdala is a key stress-responding region in our brain and plays important role in anxious situations. It's known that high amygdala activity is associated with depression and anxiety disorders (Siegle et al., 2002).

The good news is that mindfulness practice can actually shrink the size of amygdala and increase our stress reactivity threshold.

Recent research performed by Taren and colleagues shows a connection between long-term mindfulness practice and a decreased size of amygdala (Taren et al., 2013). By practicing mindfulness, we can change how we react to stressful situations and improve our mental and physical well-being.

"There's a connection between long-term mindfulness practice and a decreased size of the amygdala"

How long should you practice mindfulness?

According to Richie Davidson, one of the world's most renowned contemplative neuroscientists, even 1.5 hours of mindfulness practice leads to structural changes in the brain.

CONCLUSION

When you ask most people what it takes to become successful, they'll tell you that success comes from hard work. The psychology of success is often overlooked entirely. While yes, hard work is part of the equation, they are missing a large part. You can never become successful if you don't have the right mindset.

The right mindset cures everything. Your mindset will determine if you're successful or if you're unsuccessful. Your mindset will tell you that you're a failure and you should just give up or that you're on the right track to success. Which voice are you listening too?

Becoming an entrepreneur will be the hardest challenge of your life because you're becoming a different person than everyone else. When that happens, you will question yourself. Are you on the right path? Why don't you just work for someone else? If you continue to ask yourself these questions, you will lose. When you have the right mindset, no matter what you face, you will come out the other side.

The key to developing a growth mindset is to

understand why "fake it until you make it" is actually quite effective — it results in small wins, which then lead to genuine confidence.

That is exactly what you should do: focus on creating small wins through changing your habits. Make daily "micro quotas" (10 minutes of working out a day) that are so easy you can't say no.

In short, nail it then scale it. Over time, this creates a key trait in the growth mindset: a passion for learning rather than the need for approval.

Initial progress creates the desire to move forward. The innate mindset is what stops most people from starting ("I'm not a fit person..."), but the growth mindset will blossom after just a few small wins prove, "Hey, I can definitely do this."

It is a useful reminder that the things we want need to be claimed. They aren't a given for anyone. You don't receive an education, you claim it. You don't receive athletic success, you claim it. You don't receive mastery in your work, you claim it.

Do not go yet; One last thing to do

If you enjoyed this book or found it useful I'd be very grateful if you'd post a short review on Amazon. Your support really does make a difference and I read all the reviews personally so I can get your feedback and make this book even better.

Thanks again for your support!

www.ingramcontent.com/pod-product-compliance
Lightning Source LLC
Chambersburg PA
CBHW050726030426
42336CB00012B/1437